~~~

The Rebel and the Rabbi's Son

The Rebel and the Rabbi's Son

Finding My Soul
Beyond the Tribe

Israel "Izzy" Eichenstein

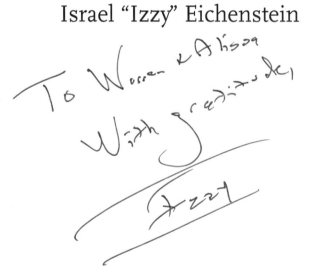

To Warren & Alison
With gratitude,
Izzy

Library of Congress CIP data applied for.

Copyright © 2013 by Israel Eichenstein. All rights reserved.
Printed in the United States of America. Except as permitted under
the United States Copyright Act of 1976, no part of this publication
may be reproduced or distributed in any form or by any means, or
stored in a database or retrieval system, without the prior written
permission of the publisher.

1 2 3 4 5 6 7 8 9 0/0 9 8 7 6 5 4 3 2 1

ISBN 13/978-0-9885063-0-5

Interior design and production: Robert S. Tinnon Design

Cover design by: Sam Kuo

Wrigley Field photo by: Jason Howell

To order additional copies of this book visit our Web site:
www.http://rabbisson.com

CONTENTS

CONTENTS

ACKNOWLEDGMENTS

This is the story of my life, Israel Eichenstein. My immediate and extended family are descendants through my father of the Zhidachov Chasidic dynasty, originating in the town of Ziditshoyv (as known in Yiddish; or Zhydachiv in Ukrainian), Galicia (a province of the former Austro-Hungarian Empire). The Zhidachov dynasty, founded by Rebbe Tzevi Hirsch Eichenstein, reigns supreme in the highly religious Chasidic world. After immigrating to America, members of our family founded new communities of the Zhidachov dynasty in Brooklyn, New York; Monticello, New York; Chicago, Illinois; London, England; and in Israel where even today they thrive and continue to live lives that are in many ways similar to those of their ancestors in the 1700s.

On my mother's side, there was just as imposing a family heritage, as we are direct descendants of the Novominsk Chasidic dynasty, originally from Minsk Mazowiecki, Poland. I wrote this book in an attempt to understand my journey and to assist others who grew up in fundamentalist communities and feel lost, lonely, scared, and scarred by rejection. Maybe you have felt that you could not express who you are or that you are unable to find your true vision for the life you want. Maybe you don't have faith in yourself. Finding and trusting who you are is the journey to your Promised Land.

I am a rabbi's son, a rabbi's grandson, a rabbi's great-grandson, and a rabbi's great-great-grandson. I have more rabbis in my family than you can count, all ultra-Orthodox, except my father of blessed memory, who was a blend of Orthodox and ultra-Orthodox.

My story is about leaving a holy rabbinical family and finding my path to heaven by going down a different road, learning that not everything called *holy* is holy, and that you don't have to feel like a sinner if you take your own path. In fact, the greatest act of faith is finding out who you really are. That is true redemption. We have to find our own reasons why we are here on this beautiful planet.

Thank you to my beautiful, soulful Rita, who has helped me in so many ways, not the least of which is believing in me. She came into my life when it was dark and storms were swirling all around. Then she pulled up the shades of my soul and the sun came brightly shining in; she has helped create magic in my life.

To my amazing children, my David, Joshua, and Deanie, you are the greatest gifts a father can have in life. You are true shining lights that radiate joy with great wisdom and depth. Erin, my beautiful daughter-in-law, your presence in the family has brought us great joy and we are enriched by all that is you. To my children and future grandchildren, find your own path to your own personal truth. Think for yourself, trust your own vision, and have faith in who you are. If you get stuck along the way, I have learned that kindness and love can unlock any door in life.

To those of you from fundamentalist backgrounds who want to get out: have faith in yourself. You can find your own path to Heaven. There is not just one door. I wish you all well in your journey through the freedom door. It is tempting to stay where you can hide and cover your pain, and I know it is much easier not to rock the boat. I am not a rebel by nature. My path out was a choice I made after experiencing my family's rigid terms of acceptance. I could not stay on their one-way street and abide by their unbending religious contract. I had to roll down my windows; I had to show faith in myself and discover that I was all right on my own terms. It had to be real for me; it had to be my own road.

Sadly, this freedom has a price. In my case, most of my family stopped talking to me. I was written off; old religious friends I grew up with now greet me superficially, at best. But it's all right with me; it has all been all worth it. Heaven is finding yourself and finding new friends who love and accept you for who you are. You wake up every day being real, talking in your own voice. You have finally found your way out of exile.

May all of you be blessed in finding your own voice, your own magic. God does not have an unlisted number. Sadly, too many people behave and believe as they are the only ones who have God's direct and private line.

Thank you to a group of incredible people in my life: Dennis and Sue Prager, Elli Wohlgelernter, Jan and Bonnie Goldstein, Jon and Lilli Bosse, Jerry and Carin Katz, Paul Rosenthal and Elaine Hantman, Tova Yellin, Shifra and Peter Bemis, Lew and Judi Rudzki, Steve and Sandra Josephson, Warren and Alissa Roston, Michael and Shelly Blumenfeld, David Friend, Ted Gluck, Susan Young, Russ and Jeri Jones, Harvey Kibel, Allan Jonas, Jim and Paula McDonald.

I want to thank Rita's cousins, Hadassa Ben Itto, Nira and Motti Kfir, Shirly and Dania Amar, and Efrat and Aaron Yehene, who welcomed me into the family and gave me a family environment that is accepting without preconditions.

To my Temple Emanuel clergy: Rabbi Laura Geller, Rabbi Jonathan Aaron, and Cantor Yonah Kliger. Thanks also to Rabbi Jill Zimmerman and her husband, Ely Zimmerman; Paul Beck; David Bolduc; Warren Mullisen; Frances Smith, and Jan Lee for their friendship.

Collectively, I want to thank all my friends at Temple Emanuel who opened the door to this wandering Jew, and to my baseball teammates: you guys are the best; let's keep winning and laughing at the same time.

A special thank you to Beth Lieberman and to Pat Kramer. I could not have gotten this book off the ground without your guidance, wisdom, superb editing skills, and encouragement. And to Lynette Padwa, the co-maestro, who has been a tireless and very devoted researcher and a magical wordsmith. You were the glue that held the project together and turned my long-running dream of having my journey put into book form. It was an honor to work with you, and your dedication to my dream will always have my deep appreciation.

Last but not least, thank you to PJ for your friendship, being a son of a minister, growing up as you did in a fundamentalist family, and finding your own wings in which you soared to record-breaking achievements—you served as my inspiration.

To my extended family, I wish you well. If you read this book, my doors are not closed to you: they never were and they never will be. I send you all greetings of peace with words from the weekday blessing *Sim Shalom*: "You and your families should all be granted peace, goodness, blessings, grace, lovingkindness and compassion."

~~~

Some of the names and places have been changed
to protect the innocent . . . . and the not so innocent.

PROLOGUE:
PURE AND IMPURE

The worst insult you can give someone in the Orthodox Jewish community is to call them *apikoros,* heretic. Many times I wonder how different my life would have been had my *zaide* (grandfather in Yiddish) been around during my lifetime. Tolerance, which he believed in, should not brand you an apikoros, as I have been branded: someone who won't share in the world to come.

They called America *treife medinah*—an "impure land." In the early 1900s, the Orthodox rabbis of Europe may have differed on many things but on one point they agreed: Jews must not emigrate to the United States. The rabbis had already seen what happened when pious immigrants stepped foot on American soil: they quickly abandoned the strict observance of Jewish law. These Jews assimilated. They intermarried. Jewish traditions that had endured for three millennia were forgotten within a year or two. So focused were the rabbis on keeping Jews away from America that they failed to grasp the anti-Semitism that was spreading across Europe after World War I. My father, Rabbi Moses Eichenstein, of blessed memory, once admitted, "If they had encouraged the Jews to leave Europe, it could have saved millions of lives." Instead, the rabbis warned their communities, "Don't go to America or you won't be Jewish anymore."

But my father's father, Yehoshua Heschel Eichenstein, did go. In the 1920s he left Chodorow (not far from the Russian-Polish border) and settled smack in the center of the treife medinah, Chicago, Illinois. Immigrating almost cost him his marriage because his father-in-law was furiously opposed to the move. Like millions before him, my zaide didn't know a word of English. He, too, was a rabbi, a member of the Chasidic Eichenstein dynasty. Years later, he would become the first Chasidic rabbi of Chicago, known as the "Zhidachov Rebbe."

All Chasidic dynasties are directly descended from the Baal Shem Tov, the charismatic teacher and healer who founded the movement in the Ukraine during the first half of the eighteenth century. Members of these dynastic families are considered royalty, elevated almost to the point of sainthood, within the ultra-Orthodox world. The men become rabbis, seers, Torah scholars, and community leaders, and the women devote their lives to sustaining the community.

By the time Zaide emigrated to the United States, several distinct groups within the Jewish community had taken shape. Ultra-Orthodox; Modern Orthodox; and non-Orthodox groups, including the Reform movement (begun in Germany during the Enlightenment) and Conservative Jews, who held fast to many traditions but were more relaxed when it came to applying them to modern life. None of these groups, for the most part, got along very well with each other. As with most religions, each claimed that the others either were not pious enough or were too rigid and intolerant. Regardless of the type of Judaism they practiced—and despite the warnings of their rabbis—thousands of Jews emigrated to America around the same time Zaide did.

Many left Poland and Russia to escape the increasingly perilous existence in Europe. My father often told the story of how his entire community once had to evacuate at a moment's notice and walk all night to the neighboring town to avoid becoming victims of a pogrom. But some Jewish families were lured by the *goldeneh medinah* (the golden land)—they wanted to improve their material life.

In the United States, the Jewish immigrants continued to harbor the rivalries and distrust that had divided them in the Old World.

Yet the challenges of forging a life in America pushed a few to consider new alliances. When Zaide moved to Chicago, it was one of the leading Reform rabbis of that city who helped him settle in and find a home, and establish the relationships that became the seeds of his Chasidic congregation. The friendship between the two men, had it happened today, would be scandalous. Back then—and today—ultra-Orthodox Jews do not as a general rule associate with members of the other branches of Judaism; especially those aligned with Reform Judaism. Then—and now—they considered the Reform movement to be "ruined" Judaism.

The only reason I know about the bond of friendship between Zaide and the Reform rabbi is because my father's conscience moved him to confide in me. I was already an adult when he pulled me aside and whispered, "Your brother or extended family would never acknowledge or believe what I'm going to tell you, but I was with your zaide when this happened." His urgent tone reminded me of a CIA operative delivering secret intelligence data.

"I was twelve years old when my father took me with him to meet the Reform rabbi who had helped him in his early days in Chicago. The Reform rabbi's daughter was getting married, and my father wished to give him a *mazel tov* (good luck). He was so grateful to this generous man that he wanted to make a public gesture." My father's eyes gleamed, challenging me to defy this stunning news: A Chasidic Rabbi went in person to wish a Reform rabbi a mazel tov at his daughter's wedding!

I understood the outrage that would have rippled through Zaide's community if it happened in today's closed-off, ultra-Orthodox Jewish world upon hearing of this event. My heart flooded with affection for this man I never met, who had died years before I was born. Even today, Orthodox rabbis probably cross the street to avoid such a man. With enough acts like that, you could end up becoming an *apikoros*, a heretic, someone who won't have a share in the world to come. Someone like me.

CHAPTER 1

LEARN, LEARN, *DAVEN, DAVEN*

E verything revolved around prayers or "davening." We said a prayer when we opened our eyes in the morning and when we shut them at night. We said a prayer over meals, and specific prayers over individual foods. Over an apple, one prayer. Over a cookie, another. One prayer for a glass of water, a different prayer for a glass of Coke.

Some of the prayers were beautiful, like the *Modeh Ani*, the morning prayer:

I thank You, living, enduring King, for You have returned my soul within me in kindness, great is Your faithfulness.

Some were talismans, like the Traveler's Prayer:

May it be Your will, Eternal One, our God and the God of our ancestors, that You lead us toward peace, emplace our footsteps towards peace, guide us toward peace, and make us reach our desired destination for life, gladness, and peace.

The prayer I probably said more often than any other, especially when I was little, was the *Asher Yatzar*:

Blessed is He who has formed man in wisdom and created in him many orifices and many cavities. It is obvious and known before Your throne of glory that if one of them were to be ruptured or one of them obstructed, it would be impossible for a man to survive and stand before You. Blessed are You that heals all flesh and does wonders.

Before and after each trip to the bathroom, I said the *Asher Yatzar.*

Every morning when I woke up, I fastened a yarmulke to my head with a bobby pin and put on a fringed holy garment called *tzitzit*, which was to be worn at all times under my shirt. I began my day by reciting the morning prayers from a prayer book known as *siddur.* These prayers lasted fifteen to twenty-five minutes, unless it was *Shabbat,* the Sabbath, or a festival day, in which case they stretched for two or three hours. I attended prayer services three times a day, every day of the week.

As an observant Orthodox Jew, my entire life was lived on the Torah Clock. In its most limited sense, Torah refers to the Five Books of Moses: Genesis, Exodus, Leviticus, Numbers, and Deuteronomy. But Torah can also refer to the entire Jewish bible (known to non-Jews as the Old Testament and to Jews as the *Tanakh,* or Written Torah). In its broadest sense, the word *Torah* encompasses the whole body of Jewish law and teachings.

Serious Orthodox students (which I was expected to become) study Torah eight to ten hours a day at a yeshivah or religious school. The traditional structure of yeshivah study was developed to educate young men in nineteenth-century Eastern Europe, with the goal of strengthening their faith in and service to God. This yeshivah model is still venerated today, and all top yeshivot in Israel and the United States aim for that ideal Torah environment. The goal for a serious yeshivah student is to completely immerse himself in the study of Torah. Ultra-Orthodox Jews believe that personal growth through the study and strict observance of the Torah is indispensable and the only way to lead an authentic Jewish life.

One of the first books an Orthodox child receives in school is a copy of the *halakhah*, or Jewish law. It is essentially a rule book for life. How detailed is the halachah? I once knew a psychotherapist who used it to help cure people of obsessive-compulsive disorder. "You like rules?" he'd ask his patients. "You like laws? Go get this book. It's so specific, it'll drive you sane."

Prayers and the halachah encircle every human action in the Orthodox world. The only activities for which there are no prayers or halakhic rules are recreational—baseball, football, going to the movies. For a majority of Orthodox Jews, this life works. They believe their purpose on earth is to follow the halachah, study Torah, have children, and raise God-fearing people who will carry on the Jewish traditions and laws. From birth until death, with *bar mitzvah* ceremonies, weddings, and funerals marking the passage of years, this is the ultra-Orthodox universe.

From a very early age, I desperately wanted to be at home and at peace in this world. Yet I didn't feel it. I didn't know why I was the odd boy out, but in hindsight, I can see that the clash of cultures I grew up in probably affected my ability to follow this narrow path. Why else would I, alone, among all the children in my huge postwar generation, be so susceptible to the lure of American girls, music, and baseball? It had to be because I was the first child in my family, for as many generations back as anyone could remember, to be raised among non-Orthodox Jews. This was not my parents' plan, but it is how our lives unfolded.

～～～

My grandfather's move to the United States had not dulled his adherence to Orthodox law despite what his father-in-law had feared. Zaide dressed as Hasidic men still do, in black, with a long coat, plain white shirt, and stiff, wide-brimmed black hat. He had a beard, which in the 1920s was long but not yet white. At first he founded a *shtibel*, or small synagogue or *shul*, but by the 1930s, Zaide had become the rabbi at a larger, ultra-Orthodox synagogue in Chicago known as the Austrian Galician (A.G.) shul. Housed in a red brick building, with tall, white columns and arched windows, A.G. was absolute in its adherence to Orthodox law. In that spirit, the shul had no choir, but Zaide and the A.G. congregants hired Metropolitan Opera star Richard Tucker to be the cantor on the High Holy Days. In his gorgeous tenor he would chant the prayers, treating the A.G. congregation to a Met-level performance that helped lift the souls of the shul's mostly poor working-class members.

The Austrian Galician shul was located on Chicago's West Side, the hub of the Jewish community until the 1950s, when most of that population migrated thirty miles across town to the North Side of the city. Zaide's congregants were recent immigrants from Eastern Europe. They could have chosen to join a Reform synagogue, but instead they stuck to their ultra-Orthodox roots. The Reform congregations of the 1920s and 1930s were much more theologically liberal than they are today—they were closer to Unitarians, striving to blend in with American culture. In general, the Reform Jews were also wealthier than the ultra-Orthodox. Resisting assimilation in order to respect the Orthodox ways, the members of Zaide's congregation were willing to forego most of the financial opportunities America offered.

But the Great Depression forced many of the shul's congregants into conflict with some of Orthodoxy's core beliefs. The most sacred of these had to do with the Shabbat. *Shabbat*, the day of rest, is the heart of Jewish life. Its purpose is to remind human beings that we are not the creator, God is. We are commanded to rest for one day a week as He did after creating the universe. Orthodox Jews take the commandment literally. On Saturdays, the Orthodox are required to halt all work—their jobs, their household chores, driving, even switching on electric lights. My grandfather's congregants were not well-off to begin with, and the Depression pushed many of them into near-poverty. If someone was lucky enough to have a job and it involved working on Saturday, observing Shabbat had to take a back-seat to feeding their family. For the ultra-Orthodox elders, this was blasphemy. Zaide felt differently. He boldly held Shabbat services for any congregant, including those who went to work directly following the closing prayers. He was one of the very few Chasidic rabbis in the United States to provide such a service.

Zaide and his wife had three sons and a daughter. My father, Moses Eichenstein, was the youngest of the boys. All three sons were studying to be rabbis. As a male members of a Chasidic dynasty, that was their only career option. The men did not work for a living; they and their families were supported by their community. At sixteen, preparing for his eventual role as a rabbi, my father began to translate Zaide's sermons from Yiddish into English so that the Jewish American children could understand them. In 1942, he met and married my mother, Sarah Perlow. They had my brother and sister and, much later, me.

My mother's family was also a Chasidic dynasty, and her father, Rabbi Perlow, had been revered throughout Eastern Europe. In the early 1900s, he was the Chief Rabbi of Warsaw, known as the *Novominsker Rebbe*, and was a dominant figure in that city's Jewish community. Every week, hundreds of people would line up around the block to request Rabbi Perlow's advice, seek his blessing, and ask for wisdom. He was considered a "Royal Rebbe," meaning a sage and community leader. When he walked into a room, people stood. My mother grew up in this rarified atmosphere, in a family of thirteen siblings who dwelled in the midst of the vast Jewish community of pre-World War II Warsaw.

Among the children who often sat at the dinner table alongside my mother was her first cousin, Abraham Joshua Heschel, who would later become a world-famous philosopher and civil rights activist. Heschel considered Rabbi Perlow to be one of his most significant spiritual influences and would later recall him as "the ideal *y'rei shamayim*" (pious man). Heschel's biographers called Perlow "the patron of [Heschel's] inmost identity."[1] Heschel, whose family lived only a few blocks from the Perlow home, visited often to talk with Rabbi Perlow and listen to conversations among the city's religious leaders, who were frequent guests as well. Some of the Perlow family, including my mother and cousin Abraham, escaped to London before the Nazis invaded Poland, but most of the Perlow relatives perished in the Holocaust.

In the 1940s and 1950s, my family lived on Chicago's West Side, where Zaide's synagogue was located and where the Orthodox community resided. The large extended family of Eichensteins and Perlows all lived within a few blocks of one another. The oldest child in my generation was a cousin eighteen years my senior, and the youngest child was me. When Zaide was felled by a stroke in the early 1940s, my father inherited his congregation.

In 1958, when I was six years old, Dad moved his synagogue from the ultra-Orthodox West Side to the non-Orthodox North Side. As my father later explained, "In the late 1950s, when I was ordained as a rabbi, I went to the head Orthodox rabbi and asked, 'Can I take a congregation that does not have an Orthodox bent?' And I was given permission to do so."

"But why did you want to?" I asked him

"I didn't have a choice. The Orthodox community was not able to support the synagogue, so we moved it to the North Side and combined it with a non-Orthodox synagogue called *Beth Israel*. That's why its name is A.G. Beth Israel."

Because my father accepted this post, he was able to make a good living. The members of the new A.G. Beth Israel congregation, being non-Orthodox, were not required to forego work in order to devote their lives to studying Torah. They seized the opportunities

---

1. Edward K. Kaplan, and Samuel H. Dresner, *Abraham Joshua Heschel, Prophetic Witness* (Yale University Press, 1998).

offered by the booming postwar economy. These men and women were comfortably middle class, and some were wealthy. All were eager to support their new synagogue with plenty of funding, including a generous salary for the rabbi and his family. The Eichensteins and Perlows who stayed in the old West Side neighborhood were appalled that Dad had moved and was now living among nonreligious Jews and serving as head of a non-Orthodox synagogue. Perhaps my father hoped that when enough years had passed, their fury would subside. "Hope for a miracle," the Talmud says, "but don't depend on one."

~~~

My father's new congregation filled a 1,200-seat synagogue on the High Holy Days. Nobody in it was Orthodox except him and my mother. The congregants had been Depression kids—they barely knew a word of Hebrew and next to nothing about Judaism. Many years later, when my father was in his eighties and retired, I could make him laugh by reciting the names of almost half the membership of that congregation. I remember them clearly because they spoiled me and treated me like a prince. When one member, Louis Goodman, asked me what I wanted for my bar mitzvah present, I naively replied, "A color TV!" I had no idea how rare and expensive they were at the time. The next thing I knew, a big box arrived at the front door, courtesy of Mr. Goodman. The Zenith color TV was enthusiastically received by me and even enjoyed by my parents.

We lived in a graceful and spacious two-story Georgian house, but it was not ostentatious. Dad abhorred any flaunting of wealth. The home was strictly kosher, with two kitchens and two sets of dishes. My mother had excellent taste and acted as decorator, installing refined yet understated furnishings and art, including plenty of family photographs. Mom considered herself to be an elegant lady, and all who knew her agreed. She was also extremely mod-

7

est: you would never see her in short sleeves, shorts, or pants. But she always looked beautiful, and her dresses were fashionable and flattering. My mother was a warm and generous woman, well suited to being a *rebbetzin*—the wife of a rabbi. She was exceptionally loving but very emotional, and she would cry at the drop of a hat. Like many people in our community, Mom never truly recovered from the losses of the Holocaust. With the exception of her larger-than-life father, who had died in the early 1930s, she never spoke about anyone in her family.

My mother was extremely observant, and if I close my eyes and think of her, I see her sitting at my father's synagogue with her prayer book open, reciting every word of the prayers along with him. Men and women sat together, a proximity that was forbidden by the Orthodox. My mother never felt entirely comfortable with the mingling of the sexes, so she would sit alone in a front pew. The congregants were sensitive to her situation and left three or four seats empty on either side of her. It was very convenient when I was a boy, because her little Izzy could sit right next to her. I was the baby of the family, and people often told me that I was Mom's favorite. I was born when she was almost forty years old, and she spoiled me terribly, much to the consternation of my older sister and cousins. I loved it, of course, and throughout my life, my mom was always my most devoted champion.

My brother and sister never attended services in the new synagogue. My sister was ten years older than me and went to live in New York shortly after our move to the North Side. My brother Jake, who was eleven when we moved, stayed home for the first year, but the new congregation confused him. He was so disturbed by the environment that he sought guidance from one of our high-powered relatives, a man who today is one of the world's most venerated ultra-Orthodox rabbis. With my father's blessing, my brother called this man, whose instructions were unequivocal: "If you want to be a true Eichenstein, you must go to a real yeshivah." Jake waited until after he became bar mitzvah, then packed his bags and moved to an ultra-Orthodox yeshivah in the Bensonhurst section of Brooklyn. He flourished there, and returned home to Chicago only twice a year for the Jewish holidays.

My brother's departure deepened my uneasy feeling that all the other Eichenstein and Perlow offspring—the cousins and my brother and sister—were on the "A" team with the ultra-Orthodox community, whereas I was now on the "B" team. After we moved I still saw my first cousins frequently, but by the time I was in third grade I was aware that I had very little in common with them. Their father, my dad's brother, was a rabbi and never failed to greet me with the standard Chasidic query: "What Torah portion are you learning?"

"I'm learning about *Tzav* (Torah portion)," I might respond. In truth, I knew more about Ernie Banks's batting stance than anything about the Torah. "Ah," my uncle would say, squinting down at me intently. "So what does Rashi say about this section? What did the Talmud say about that?"

I was bombarded with questions as if it was a game show, but it wasn't fun like a game show because I never had the right answer. I was uninterested in any portion of the Torah. Chasidic men spent their entire life studying it. I studied sports. If my uncle had asked me to recite the Chicago Cubs lineup or stats regarding the Chicago Bears, I would have astonished him with my knowledge and feats of memory. Instead, every encounter was a humiliating public Torah test that I usually failed.

On Saturdays I would sit with my mother alone in the pew, listening to my Orthodox father deliver his sermon to the non-Orthodox congregation, who treated me with respect and kindness. Later I would visit with ultra-Orthodox relatives and friends from the old neighborhood and overhear their whispers: *I've never met a group of Jews who know less about the religion than the members of Rabbi Eichenstein's synagogue. . . . The rabbi is a nice man, but in his synagogue men and women sit together. . . . They use a microphone on Shabbat on Sat-*

urday. . . . That kid of his is going to be so confused he won't know his left arm from his right. Yet when they needed money (which was often, since none of the men worked), these same family members did not hesitate to ask my father for it, and he always complied.

The many contradictions in my father's life crowded my young mind. He had an Orthodox prayer book. He had a huge synagogue on a big block on Chicago's North Side, much different than the modest West Side *shtibels.* Every Friday at sundown my father would lock the synagogue's parking lot and it would remain locked until Saturday night, because observant Jews do not drive on Shabbat. How, then, did everybody get to services Saturday morning? They drove and parked nearby, and no one mentioned it. Keeping the parking lot locked on Saturday was one of the terms my father had insisted upon when drawing up his agreement with the synagogue. He was not going to compromise his principles. But he still let everybody in.

In third grade I started attending an Orthodox Jewish day school. Prior to that I had attended the local public school with the children of my father's congregants. Transitioning to the Orthodox day school was a radical change for me—social life as I knew it was wiped away. In my Jewish grammar school, half the day was devoted to Judaic studies, from the Prophets to the Halakhic laws. The other half consisted of secular studies. Later there were two more short prayer services. At this new school, some of the students felt it was their duty to point out my father's transgressions, which everyone knew about since it was such a close-knit community. One classmate, whose family had also moved to the North Side, informed me, "We were all set to go to services every Shabbat with your dad, but then we saw what kind of an irreligious synagogue he has. How could he do that? We're never going there."

My mother sensed my unhappiness at the Jewish school and insisted that I attend summer classes in literature at Francis Parker School, a preppy private school on the North Shore of Chicago. I had always loved to read, and she wanted to make sure that love was nourished somehow. Unfortunately, the culture shock between Frances Parker and my Orthodox day school jolted me into further confusion.

My classmates at the new school sometimes hurt my feelings, my father's situation confused me, and weekend visits to my old West Side neighborhood felt like trips to a hostile foreign country. Fortunately, sports were my saving grace and refuge. On Saturday afternoons I still managed to watch my beloved games on TV at the homes of my sports-loving buddies from the public school, and I still played on whatever teams I could find. It's not fair to compare a baseball team to a family, but the connection that I felt to my teammates—even teammates in a pickup game at the park—was a much closer bond than I felt with any of my family members except my mom.

Before I ever joined a real baseball team I was an avid fan, especially of the Chicago Cubs, whose ups and downs I followed fanatically on my transistor radio. At night I would put it under my pillow and listen to the ball game until I fell asleep. According to Jewish law, you can listen to a TV or radio during Shabbat as long as you turn it on before sundown on Friday night and do not touch it for the next twenty-four hours. You may not, under any circumstances, turn an appliance on or off or adjust the volume until Shabbat is over.

One Friday night, when I was eight years old, I was listening to the Cubs game in bed. It was barely audible—I had forgotten to turn the volume up before the sun went down. I slid my hand under the pillow and my fingers crept toward the dial. I was scared out of my mind. My index finger touched the knob, hesitated, then twisted it up. The sound of the game swelled in my ear. The ceiling did not fall down. With that first transgression, a reluctant rebel was born.

CHAPTER 2

LOST IN TRANSLATION: NAKED LADIES AND THE BEACHES

I attended the Jewish day school until I was thirteen. I always had a large group of friends, but academically I was only mediocre. I would say that I struggled and I wasn't interested enough to try that hard. It was difficult for me to concentrate except on the ball field, where I excelled at baseball and football. I liked both, but baseball was really my game. My positions were either the outfield or third base—I was a swift runner and could hit the ball pretty well too. I played on school teams and in pickup games in my neighborhood where my teammates were the nonreligious kids who went to the Hebrew school at my dad's synagogue.

More than anything else, playing sports kept me sane during my formative years. Baseball and football were much more than a release valve for my energy or a place to focus my restless mind. In the Orthodox world, sports were not a threat. They were among the very few enjoyable activities that were not frowned upon, so I could safely throw myself into the games. I was proud of my sports ability, whereas I was not so proud of my Torah knowledge, my inattentiveness in class, and my near total lack of curiosity about Jewish subjects. Playing ball, whether in school or in my front yard, was the one reliable positive interlude in a life that seemed to be full of things I wasn't any good at.

The Orthodox tolerance toward ball playing didn't extend to playing on Shabbat, of course. That was a day of rest, which was exactly what my father was doing one Saturday when I was about ten years old. He was upstairs napping, and I was in the front yard tossing a ball with a friend. There were two synagogues on my block, my father's and another that was ultra-Orthodox. On this particular Saturday, an Orthodox rabbi was walking by on his way to services and saw me playing baseball. Naturally, he knew who I was.

"Does your father know you're out here playing?" he demanded. "You should be ashamed of yourself. It's Shabbat. I'm going to call your father and tell him about it." Chances are my dad did know and looked the other way, yet this rabbi's threat scared the daylights out of me. The incident was emblematic of the tightrope I always felt I was walking, never knowing which move might send me hurtling into a frigid pool of my family's condemnation. I put down the baseball and scooted indoors, waiting out the rest of the afternoon in my bedroom, but my father never mentioned it. Looking back, I suspect that he had a much more sympathetic attitude toward me than he was willing to outwardly acknowledge.

If my parents' disapproval terrified me, the Chasidic community's disapproval seemed to terrify them. They were especially intimidated by the leaders of the large Perlow and Eichenstein families, who were prominent and influential, not only in Chicago and New York, but also in the Orthodox communities around the world.

A current friend of mine told me that he had his bar mitzvah ceremony at one of the many Eichenstein synagogues in the country. "You uncle was the scariest man I ever met," he told me.

Without exaggeration, the names Eichenstein and Perlow were tantamount to Kennedy—a "royal family" in that very small part of the world. As children of revered Chasidic rabbis, my parents endured relentless criticism from the extended family, all of whom looked down on them for having "sold out" by being the rabbi and rebbetzin of a non-Orthodox synagogue. Of course, they accepted the generous financial help my dad graciously gave them and ignored the fact that it came from the source that they disparaged. They did not disparage my father (at least not that I know of) but greatly disdained his choice of pulpit.

Occasionally our home would be visited by one of the Talmudic gunslingers, as I used to call them—the men with the big beards who carried the holy name of the family. Their presence in our house had the same gravity-shifting effect as a visit from the pope would have on a Catholic family. My parents, whom I was used to seeing as authority figures revered by their congregation, suddenly seemed small, unsure, and too eager to please. Most of the gunslinger rabbis were quite harsh in their demeanor—in fact, they were menacing. Their effect on Mom and Dad made them even scarier to me.

Whenever we attended a large function such as a wedding, I got to see just how imposing the gathered clan was. The head table would feature a lineup of my cousins and uncles, men in black suits and large drumlike fur hats called *shtreimels*, which they wore throughout the event. A few were young and arrogant, but most were older, their long, white beards giving them a biblical ferocity. Their dour expressions, no matter how joyous the occasion, signaled that they carried the weight of the world on their shoulders. Maybe in their own minds, they did. No wonder my parents were intimidated by them.

Given this background, it's not surprising that despite my father's non-Orthodox congregation, he and my mother wanted me schooled in a traditional Orthodox style. The teachers at the Jewish day schools I attended were all male, and most were ordained rabbis who had survived the Holocaust in Europe. They spoke with thick Yiddish accents and wore the standard black suits and long beards. The teachers told my parents that I was very smart but was not applying myself. I loved to read but had a great deal of trouble focusing, not only on Jewish subjects but also on secular studies. A large part of the curriculum was moral instruction, which always came down to a simple command: study Torah and be a serious student. Fun was never mentioned. Enjoyment and entertainment were frivolous. The goal of school and life was to become a "Torah-true" person. Everything we learned was meant to prepare us for being a *yeshivah bocher*, a true yeshivah student.

Although my eyes usually glazed over during the classroom sermons on morality, I do remember one lecture that was delivered just before school let out for the summer in seventh grade. As the warm June air wafted over the hot skin of two dozen thirteen-year-old males, the teacher paced and glared, issuing vacation instructions in his Yiddish accent: "I vant all the boys to know that you cannot go to the bitches because the bitches are very, very bad for you. You gonna see the *knockedeh* (naked) ladies at the bitches. Stay avay from the knockedeh ladies and the bitches!"

Stay away from the naked ladies and the beaches! I started snickering and soon the whole class was giggling along with me. I laughed so hard that I got kicked out of class and spent the rest of the hour in the hall, fantasizing about what I would do with a knockedeh lady at a bitch if I was lucky enough to find one.

In fact, I had already seen knockadeh ladies—in photos, anyway. That year I had become friends with Stevie, a classmate, whose family was non-Orthodox. He was not a bad kid, but I could tell that when he came over, my mother was not happy. That was all right with me. I preferred to go to his house where we could pore over his dad's *Playboy* magazines. Not surprisingly, when we weren't looking at the *Playboys,* we were thinking about them. One day, Stevie called me up to rave about the latest issue. "You can't imagine how fantastic Ursula Andress looks in a bikini. Unbelievable. It's just unbelievable." When he hung up a few minutes later, I heard a second click, and my stomach dropped. My mom had been listening.

She instantly came into my room looking as if she had seen a ghost. Her son reading *Playboy?*

"I'm disappointed in you," she said, her voice sounding a little strangled. But she quickly rallied. "This Stevie is a bad influence, Izzy. You're hanging out with the wrong people. You're going in the wrong direction. This is not the way a future yeshivah boy talks!" She didn't like Stevie, she didn't like his family. He didn't come from the right stuff.

But the bonds of friendship are strong and access to *Playboy* makes them even stronger. A week later I was back at Stevie's house, and he was showing me Miss Andress's bikini photos. His description had not done her justice! Eventually we managed to tear ourselves away long enough to go outside for a while, at which point I realized I had lost my glasses. Stevie's mom found them a few days later—in the *Playboy*. She thought it was hilarious. She was as cool and funny as my family was uptight, and she called me herself to tell me.

Somehow that story got out, and sure enough it got back to my parents, who were not only disappointed but also now publicly humiliated. I sensed that I was walking on ever thinner ice with the family, but for the immediate future, I was safe from extreme measures. I was about to become bar mitzvah, and everything would have to be put on hold until after that.

CHAPTER 3

BAR MITZVAH AND BEYOND

B ar mitzvah ceremonies, in the Orthodox world, are seen as serious and also joyous occasions where the boy comes of age. This means that he is required to observe all the *mitzvot* (613 commandments) that adult males observe, including prayers three times a day as well as an increase in daily Torah study. Bar mitzvah boys were expected to mature to a higher level—to leave behind their childish ways and embrace a much more serious demeanor and new enthusiasm for Torah learning. If there are twelve steps to becoming a serious Torah-observant Orthodox Jew, the bar mitzvah step is certainly one of the main ones. Yet, as I much as I realized the gravity of the event and wanted very much to transition along with my peers, I just couldn't get there. I felt nothing.

Unfortunately for me, the bar mitzvah ceremony of a rabbi's son, especially from the Eichenstein family, held even more expectation. There was a public aspect to it, as I would be "performing" in front of the congregation and the vast extended family. Not only would I be called up to the Torah, I would be leading the entire service, including reading the complete Torah portion and *haftarah* and leading all the prayers. Not to mention my teaching about the Torah portion, which was expected to be at the highest level of sophistication.

As the preparations unfolded, I couldn't help but notice the no-nonsense practicality with which my parents approached the inevitable religious and family conflicts that the Big Day would generate. Mom and Dad had to contend with three main issues. First, how could they hold my bar mitzvah ceremony in Dad's synagogue and also not allow the congregants to drive there? On all the other Shabbats of the year, Dad quietly looked the other way when his congregants drove to services. Since the ultra-Orthodox members of the family did not attend Dad's synagogue, they were not there to challenge him about it. But they had all been invited to services the day I became bar mitzvah. Equally urgent was my father's sincere wish that this occasion not be the reason that the entire congregation violated Shabbat.

My parents solved the problem by holding this service on an Intermediate Day during Passover. During those intermediate days, Orthodox law allows people to work, drive, use musical instruments, and in general, lead normal lives.

The second challenge was figuring out how to separate the men and the women as strict Orthodoxy requires. Dad's synagogue was not divided into two sections, and throughout the year, men and women sat and prayed together with no separation. Without missing a beat, my parents decided that they would divide the sanctuary in two by placing enormous flower arrangements down the center aisle.

The final dilemma: how could my parents coax the extended family, all Chasidic, to attend? I felt the anxious hum of their concern over this matter, but in the end, I suspect that guilt convinced a few token family members to show up. After all, they regularly accepted money from my father. Completely shunning this event would have been an act too brazenly insulting even for them.

At least I knew how to put on *tefillin*, a precise ritual that I would be required to execute flawlessly in front of the congregation. The tefillin are two small black boxes with leather straps attached to them; one box is worn on the arm, the other on the head above the hairline. Putting them on involved strapping one box on my left (non-writing) arm with the knot placed inward toward the heart, saying a prayer and winding the leather straps seven times around my bicep and forearm, placing the other box on my forehead, wrapping the strap around my middle finger three times, saying another prayer . . . it was complicated.

A few weeks prior to the bar mitzvah ceremony, my father had taken me to my cousin Velvel's home so that the older boy could show me how to do it. He was no longer a boy, actually, but a twenty-three-year-old yeshivah graduate. Torah-true to the core, Velvel would grow up to become the Zhidachov Rebbe of Chicago, where to this day, his followers and many unaffiliated but Orthodox people hold him in the highest esteem. Back then he was simply a pale young man with a sparse beard and long *peyos* (long side curls).

Velvel lived with the rest of his family in the old neighborhood. Our fathers were brothers, and both were rabbis, but Uncle Avrohom had stayed within the strictly Chasidic world. They resided in a three-story apartment building that had been donated to the family and had a little *shtibel* on the first floor. The third floor housed my father's younger sister and her three children. In between, on the second floor, lived my uncle and aunt and all their children, who were in their twenties, as well as my father's mother. Being a rabbi's widow, she was called *the Rebbitzen*, just like my mom was in our congregation. The Rebbitzen was a mysterious old lady who spoke only Yiddish. She knew exactly two words in English: "the machine," which is what she called the car. Each Chanukkah we would visit her and in Yiddish she would tell my aunt, "Give him some Chanukkah gelt." My aunt would write a check and hand it to me. My father would thank his mother profusely. And as soon as we left the building, he would ask me for the check and proceed to tear it up—my grandmother had no money, but Dad wanted her to feel as if she had given me a gift.

Although the apartment building was large, it seemed stuffy and overcrowded. There were no children my age, just a collection of cousins who seemed much older and certainly more serious than the average twenty-something. It was 1968, and the rest of the

United States was exploding with rock music, political protests, and the civil rights movement. On this Chicago block, not only did time stand still, it seemed to have reversed. It might as well have been 1928. There were people who were learning Torah on all floors at all hours of the day and night, occasionally sleeping over or staying there for several days.

My uncle had an open home and an open heart; wandering Jews traveling in search of funds for their yeshivot or who were on some kind of personal journey could find a place to rest here. In a sense, Uncle Avrohom offered a free hostel for wandering pilgrims of the ultra-Orthodox bent. He was an unusual and generous man and I remember him fondly. My uncle sponsored many refugees from the Holocaust so as to help them gain entrance visas to the United States. One in particular stands out—my future father-in-law, who was an orphaned refugee from Poland.

When we arrived at the apartment for my bar mitzvah instruction, my father pulled my cousin Velvel aside and said, "Would you teach Izzy how to put on the tefillin?" Velvel slowly walked over and looked at me with a combination of pity and disgust. Grudgingly, he showed me the basics.

The night before I became bar mitzvah, I was so nervous that I didn't sleep all night. The expectations of me felt over the top. More than 500 people were supposed to attend the event, including a few members of the extended family. The flower separation barrier looked gorgeous, and the congregants amiably took their places in the gender-appropriate sections. I had been practicing the service for many months, and I needed to, because in Orthodox bar mitzvah ceremonies, every word of Hebrew must be pronounced in its pure, unmodified form. For a thirteen-year-old it's a daunting task. In most cases, however, the bar mitzvah boy is given a little leeway even in these strict services. I would have been, too, if it weren't for my father's nemesis, the custodian of the synagogue, Mr. W. He had moved from Chicago's West Side to the city's North Side when my father did, and was placed in the same synagogue. Mr. W. was a colorful character who craved attention. On this day he got it by cutting me off and barking out the correct pronunciation every time I flubbed a Hebrew word. My biggest challenge was ignoring him and plowing ahead, which I managed to do, but it was a gut-wrenching experience I still vividly recall.

The service finally ended and the party began. There were strolling violin players, my parents seemed happy, the congregants were wishing them a mazel tov, and the extended family members stayed for the festivities. For them, stepping into Dad's synagogue was no small feat—it was as if they held their noses while having to taste a very bad meal. They seemed to survive, though, and I was unaware of any casualties or injuries to those who came. Except for me. I'm not sure that I escaped entirely unscathed.

~~~

Three months later I graduated eighth grade, which meant that it was time to select a high school. In the Orthodox world, you are given some slack until you become a bar mitzvah, but then the expectations change. If you are not getting your act together religiously, the crackdown begins. In the seventh and eighth grade of Orthodox yeshivah, the boys are observed with an eagle eye. Do they remember to say their prayers coming out of the bathroom? Do they say it with *kavanah* (intention), or do they just mumble? Are they alert to Talmudic intricacies or are they daydreamers in class? Who has been caught looking at the girls, and who seems more focused on Torah? Who shows up at shul early on Saturday morning and who comes later, having slept in? The votes are cast and the verdicts are in by mid-eighth grade: who is a serious *bocher* and who is a slacker? It was clear that I was in the latter category, given that I spent most of my time on the baseball field. But to honor my family, the school placed me in the advanced Talmud class. I was uninterested and being there was uncomfortable. I was starting to get heavy pressure from both parents to get serious, and it was at this time that my conflicts with Mom and Dad began to escalate.

Toward the end of eighth grade, my classmates and I were given tours of two Jewish high schools. The first, a coed school, was very relaxed. Boys and girls studied together, there was a nice camaraderie among staff and students, and there were a lot of fun activities. It was still Orthodox, but maybe with a small 'o.' The second choice, a yeshivah, was male-only with very long days—8 a.m. to 8 p.m. classes six days a week. To make it even stricter, the boys were housed in a dormitory where they were monitored by a *mashgiach*, a supervisor whose role was to provide a positive influence and maintain Torah standards in the dorm. After touring the coed school and the all-male yeshivah, I told my parents that I wanted to attend the coed school where the environment was more comfortable to me (cheerleaders for the basketball team didn't hurt, either). I thought I would fit right in.

My parents immediately vetoed the idea; in fact, a faster veto has never been issued. I protested strongly, but to no avail, and off I went to the yeshivah high school. I was keenly aware of the growing sense of alarm coming from my parents and the family. I was expected to focus on Jewish learning and start down the path of being a *talmud chochom*, a high achieving Torah-learned person. It was comforting, at least, that I was going to this school with a bunch of guys who were my buddies from the Jewish grammar school. Some of them were also not overly devout and I felt I could be myself with them, at least initially. We shared a lot of good times together but eventually we grew apart religiously, as they started to sense that I wasn't with the program.

In the middle of freshman year, aware of the circling vibe of disapproval and urgently wanting to please my parents, I had a brainstorm. If I had known about the Stockholm syndrome, where a prisoner identifies with his captors, I might have recognized that as a driving force behind my plan. As it was, I acted out of desperation because I could see that my dad was beginning to give me the brush-off. Was he going to disown me entirely? I needed to do something dramatic that would prove to him I was a worthy member of the family.

My friend Stevie helped me cook up the plan. Denver, Colorado, had a highly respected yeshivah at that time. I told Stevie, "If I get into Denver and become a serious yeshivah student like my brother, they'll really like me.'"

"Do it," Stevie urged, and together we composed a letter to the admissions counselor.

A week or so later, the counselor called me personally to respond. He did not mince words. "You have a reputation as a playboy," he informed me. "We do not feel that you are serious yeshivah material." I was stunned, but I didn't defend myself. The yeshivah network was wired with personal connections, so the counselor could easily have called any rabbi in Chicago and asked, "What do you know about Izzy Eichenstein?"

"He's a pretty wild kid," the reply must have come. "He plays a lot of sports, he's not a serious Torah learner, he gets involved with girls."

In retrospect, I'm glad it worked out that way. The counselor was right—not about my being wild, but about the academy in Denver possibly not being "a good fit," to use today's genteel term. At Yeshivah High School in Chicago, I had some wonderful experiences. I made great friends, including Elli, another clergy kid. Elli and I got along for a lot of reasons. We were both rabbis' sons, we both loved baseball and girls, and we were considered misfits. We were not your typical yeshivah guys. We're still friends, and I've seen Elli courageously fight his way through many challenges before moving to Israel to work as a very successful journalist and terrific father.

In ninth grade I played on the freshman football and baseball teams and enjoyed (mostly in secret) friendships with the girls who attended the nearby coed Jewish high school. I usually stayed out of trouble, except for the day a mother caught me making out with a girl at a party. She immediately called my parents. "How could a rabbi let his son behave this way?" You would think I was Hugh Hefner. But it was supposed to be a religious environment, and making out with girls was certainly not on the list of accepted behaviors.

My early Yeshivah High School years were further complicated by the presence of two rabbis who were teachers on the faculty and who happened to be my cousins. One was my old pal Velvel, who had reluctantly shown me how to wear tefillin. The other was Rabbi Naftali. Neither taught any of the classes in which I was enrolled, but I saw them all the time. These two were in charge of giving lectures on moral behavior. I don't think having me on campus assisted in their crusade. Both of them were zealots, the right-wing Bible thumpers of the school. Their favorite topic was the shameful state of American culture. Velvel liked to tell us, "The whole world is run on sex appeal." Both rabbis were always warning the students to stay away from bad magazines, bad movies, and bad influences. I can't overemphasize the word *bad*; just about everything in the secular world was considered bad or *treife*. Secular enjoyments were not only frowned upon, you were to run from them like the plague.

The irony is that I wasn't the only guy who didn't have the proper enthusiasm for the straight and narrow yeshivah road. In fact, compared to some of my classmates I was angelic. A few boys (maybe more than a few) dabbled in smoking cigarettes and marijuana and sampling non-kosher burgers at Jack's, the local burger joint. I never did any of this. But because of my cousins' scrutiny, I walked around feeling like a borderline criminal if I so much as sneezed wrong. Having Velvel and Rabbi Naftali at the school meant that the probing eye of the extended family could peer into the classroom and onto the schoolyard. They were particularly riled to hear that I was keeping company with girls on the weekends.

Between my cousins teaching at the school, the expectations heaped upon me because of my last name, and my inability to embrace the Torah-true study ethic, I felt as if a negative force field emanated from me when I walked through the campus. I couldn't ignore the vibes I picked up with what I was beginning to think of as my radar—a powerful gut instinct that, over the years, has proven to be extremely accurate.

My radar told me that my family did not approve of me or like me very much, and with a few exceptions, neither did my teachers. It was hard to operate that way. I felt as if I were at war, but I couldn't fight back because I had nothing to fight with—these people just didn't like who I was. Fortunately I had lots of friends. In the great tradition of outcasts everywhere, I used humor to deflect the pain and it made me a popular kid. But whenever I was with my extended family, the cold stares, Torah grill sessions, and palpable disapproval left me feeling sick. The day after a family get-together, I'd be depressed and physically exhausted. I didn't want to go to these functions but refusing was out of the question.

As the summer of 1968 approached, I began to breathe more easily. For the previous two years, I had attended summer camp in Wild Rose, Wisconsin, an eight-hour drive from Chicago. In June I would be heading back there again. If sports were the escape that made my daily life tolerable, Camp Moshava was the Technicolor icing on my year. A coed Zionist camp modeled after a kibbutz, Moshava served children between the ages of nine and seventeen. It was situated on a lake that was mostly nonfunctional, but we could row a boat on it and occasionally brave its freezing water. There were tremendous open spaces, playing fields, and a bonfire area where we gathered to sing Jewish and Zionist songs—there was a lot of singing. On Shabbat, all the boys wore white shirts and black pants, while the girls wore white shirts and blue skirts. When it wasn't Shabbat we wore shorts and T-shirts that got satisfyingly ragged and grimy as the weeks sped by. We slept in cabins with other kids and a few counselors, and I was free to play sports and hang out with friends of both sexes, far from my watchful cousins and embattled parents. I was popular—not that I lived for popularity, but I always had a lot of friends and was in the midst of the action. These were my people, my core group of buddies; this was where being myself was actually a good thing. I even had a girlfriend. I put the Yeshivah High School out of my mind for the entire three months.

In the fall I entered my sophomore year, cautious but optimistic. Things began fairly smoothly with classes, football practice, and games against other schools. Then, on November 12, 1968, after scoring two touchdowns and intercepting the quarterback for the third time on that day, I was tackled and broke my leg. The break was so loud that other students could hear the sound of the bone snapping. I was rushed in an ambulance to the hospital where the surgeon first recommended operating, but in the end, put my leg in a cast. The cast stayed on for the next four months until March.

It was a bad break in more ways than one. After that injury, the school year became a lot more difficult. Sports, my main escape, was no longer an option. The level of Jewish learning expected of me was increasing and my success with it was shrinking. The rabbi-teachers were confused—my lack of interest and enthusiasm really seemed to get under their skin. Near the end of the first semester, one of them pulled me aside and told me, "You have the example of your older brother, Yaakov. Follow that example. Be more like him."

Yaakov—or Jake, as he used to be known—had now been living at a right-wing yeshivah in Brooklyn for many years. Jake had informed the family shortly after moving there that he wanted to be called by his Hebrew name, Yaakov. He had a well-deserved reputation as a Talmudic scholar-in-training who studied seven days a week. I recalled my brother warmly because it was he who had taught me to play baseball and taken me to my first game. ("Worst things I ever did," he would later grouse.) Yaakov was a good person and very sincere in his beliefs, but at this point I didn't know him well. The tidbits of information I had gleaned about the Brooklyn yeshivah made it sound as if he had climbed into a time machine and landed back in Eastern Europe, circa 1900. Attending college was prohibited; newspapers and radios were hidden away. Since he had left home to attend this yeshivah, I saw him only when he returned for Passover and occasional visits.

Yaakov obviously agreed with the strict teachings of the ultra-Orthodox community where he now resided. It was a highly segregated world where men and women were not allowed to touch one another unless they were related. Rules of *tznius*, or modesty, were extremely complex and endlessly debated among the scholars. Beyond the rules about dressing, there were laws about such things as when and if a man could listen to a woman sing. It seemed to depend on whether hearing the female voice would cause the man sexual pleasure. Hymns, funeral dirges, and lullabies were usually allowed, while other types of songs were deemed too alluring. I had even read an article discussing whether gazing at a woman's little finger was acceptable. Some said it was permitted unless gazing at the pinky finger caused a man to become aroused. As a fourteen-year-old male, I could relate.

About a month after my cast came off, my brother returned home for Passover. He was kind to me, as always, but seemed more removed than ever. He certainly behaved in a more Orthodox manner than either of my parents, who for many years, had moved easily among their non-Orthodox congregants. Yaakov seemed ill at ease in our house, a place that had never really been home to him. He was a "black hatter" now, devoutly committed to the most right-wing branch of ultra-Orthodox Judaism.

One day shortly after Yaakov arrived, my family hosted guests from the synagogue for the evening meal. As they were leaving, one of the men said goodbye to my dad and then shook my mother's hand. My brother saw this, turned pale, and left the room visibly upset. Mom had no problem shaking hands with men; I had seen her do it dozens of times. What was going on here? Was I supposed to discuss this with Mom or say nothing? In the end, I didn't mention the incident to anyone, but the scene stuck in my head.

As tenth grade wound down, I felt more lost than ever. My brother was living on another planet and my sister was married off to an ordained rabbi who made zealotry in the name of ultra-Orthodox Judaism his main mission in life. My family could be very cordial to me if they thought I was on the team, but if they picked up a vibe that deviated even slightly from their religious views, they shut me down with icy stares that said, *You will not be tolerated.* I got the message but there was nothing I could do. I didn't want to be a rebel. I didn't want to be in the doghouse with my family. I wanted to belong, to be one of them. Yet I needed oxygen. I had to get out. I could hardly wait for yet another school year to finish when I would return to the one place where I could relax—Camp Moshava.

CHAPTER 4

THE SOUL-SAVING
FAMILY PLAN

R abbi Naftali called me into his office about a week before summer vacation. From across his desk he regarded me with an imperious gaze.

"Do you understand how you should behave?" he began.

"How?" I countered.

"You represent both Perlows and Eichensteins. Yet your behavior this year has been disrespectful. Why don't you take Jewish learning more seriously? Your actions reflect poorly on the family."

"Next year I'll do better," I promised.

"Why wait until next year? I can arrange to send you to a Jewish summer camp in the Catskills where serious students learn Torah and live a Torah-true life. You can make that change now, not next fall."

"I'm going to Camp Moshava, like I always do."

"That is not an appropriate camp for you."

"That's where I'm going. Camp Moshava," I repeated. I was shaken by his intrusion into this personal decision—was there any part of my life that he didn't feel was his business? But I didn't budge, and two weeks later I was on sacred ground—Wild Rose, Wisconsin.

My parents were reluctant to send me back to the coed, modern Orthodox summer camp, but they did it. Behind the scenes, however, my older sister and brother, along with Rabbi Naftali and a few of the top bosses of the family, were contacting Mom and Dad. I was rapidly becoming a bad kid, they reported—girls, music, sports, long hair, the usual litany of transgressions. I needed to be saved. They were determined to make Dad see the mistake he had made in allowing me to escape to Moshava.

The extended family liked my father, but that didn't alter the disdain they felt for him and his synagogue. His judgment was clearly suspect: witness how I was turning out. Dad was always torn between being who he was—flexible, kind, and pragmatic—and being the unbending ultra-Orthodox rebbe the extended family expected. He was tormented by the strain of this balancing act. For their part, the Eichensteins and Perlows were not impressed with Dad's leadership skills or the fact that the congregants at A.G. Beth Israel adored him.

As harsh as my father could be toward me (and my siblings), he was unfailingly gracious and warm with members of his congregation. I can recall walking with him on Saturday mornings and occasionally seeing one of his congregants mowing the lawn, which is about as bad as it gets in terms of breaking Shabbat. At the sight of my father, the offender would sheepishly say something like, "Rabbi, I'm sorry, I'm not religious." My father would respond, "Don't say that about yourself." He was supportive of all his congregants and accepting of whatever form of Judaism they were able to practice. They repaid him by enthusiastically embracing his synagogue. To the extended Eichensteins and Perlows, however, the opinions of a crowd of non-Orthodox Jews were irrelevant. All that mattered was making sure that my father kept his brood safe from the lawn-mowing hordes. Of all the members on both sides of the family, and there were scores of them, I was the only soul tempted to peek outside the ultra-Orthodox tent, at least as far as I knew.

Before I departed for Camp Moshava, I had noticed the atmosphere around my house changing for the worse. It felt the way it did when the skies were cloudy and I knew rain was moving in. My father was becoming more remote; he couldn't get over the idea that he had failed in raising me. I was the embodiment of his struggle between his family and his chosen career, but at fifteen I didn't understand that. I only knew that I needed to leave as quickly as possible. By the time I was an hour outside of Chicago, I had dismissed all thoughts of the storm brewing at home and turned my attention to reuniting with my summer friends.

On Friday, July 18, 1969, about two weeks after I arrived at camp, I was called into the office of the director. To my astonishment, my father and mother were sitting there.

"Sit down, Izzy," said the director, a gentle and diplomatic man. He looked at my mother and father, his face neutral.

"We're taking you out of camp," my father announced.

"What? Why?"

"We'll stay for Shabbat, and on Sunday we're driving you back to Chicago. We're sending you to a Torah learning camp in the Catskills."

"I'm not going."

"We're taking you out on Sunday," Dad restated.

"No. I won't leave." I felt physically ill, almost as if I were gasping for air. This was impossible, it was not happening. I would refuse. I looked at the director, who seemed nearly as upset as I was. Then I ran out of the office, telling a few friends who had gathered outside. Shock rippled through the small group and rolled back over me, hitting me in waves. How could my parents do this to me? They had burst into my territory and were now going to rip me away from the people who not only accepted me but actually liked who I was.

At sundown on Fridays, Camp Moshava ushered in Shabbat with a prayer service filled with enchanting spiritual melodies that were usually a highlight of my week. On this night, I was an emotional basket case. I refused to sit next to my father, positioning myself across the room and aiming a beam of fury at him that could have drilled through the crust of the earth. Dad sat rigidly, his arms crossed over his chest as if he were protecting himself from the blows of a boxer. After a few minutes, my counselor came over to me and whispered, "Why don't you go sit with your dad?"

I stiffly moved to sit beside my father and saw that tears were trickling down his cheeks. Maybe there was a chance he would change his mind . . . .

Saturday was a relaxed time filled with low-key activities centered around services, meals, and socializing. Word had gotten out that on Sunday I was leaving. My friends and camp counselors asked me why I had to go and I had no answer. It felt like a punishment, but what had I done wrong? I made an effort to change my parents' minds, and so did the director, knowing how deeply unhappy I was. But nothing would move my mother and father.

Sunday, July 21, Neil Armstrong took man's first steps on the Moon. I recall the campers talking about it that morning as I packed my suitcase. The entire camp lined the long driveway to say goodbye to me. It was almost like a funeral. My parents' black car rolled slowly down the tree-lined road, everybody waved, and I could see two of my close friends wiping their eyes. Then we turned onto the main highway, and Camp Moshava melted into the woods.

$$\approx\approx$$

I did not talk to my parents for the entire eight-hour drive back to Chicago. I was home for two days, and then Mom and Dad put me on a plane to New York City. When I landed, I was to go directly to Port Authority and board a bus to Monticello, New York, where my brother would meet me and take me to the Torah learning camp he was attending.

I did exactly as I was told.

Yaakov greeted me happily—he was thrilled to finally get the chance to show me how joyous and satisfying the Torah-true lifestyle could be. He knew I had to be dragged there, but he remained optimistic. We bumped along a rutted asphalt road that smelled like hot tar. My brother made small talk, asking innocent questions such as, "How's Dad?" I gave him a thousand-mile stare and didn't reply. Finally we arrived at the camp. The scene before me shook me out of my funk and threw me into disbelief. It was a mess.

While Camp Moshava had not been Club Med, it had been clean, relatively modern, and well maintained. It was the type of place where cupboards would be stocked with food and towels would be available. This place, which I instantly dubbed Camp Stone Age, was the equivalent of an old movie theater with half the seats missing. There was no grass, just dirt and weeds. Even the trees seemed mossy and unkempt. A small swimming pool featured a diving board that appeared to be hanging from a single bolt. The cabins looked dilapidated. And the kids . . . there were lots of them, from eight-year-olds to teenagers, almost all wearing *peyos* and *tzitzit*. They were playing ball and running around looking quite happy, their peyos bouncing from beneath baseball caps. I felt as if I had landed on the moon, just like Neil Armstrong. Except that Armstrong would get to leave after a few days. And he got to wear a cool spacesuit instead of tzitzit.

"I know you loved Camp Moshava, Izzy, but look: they're playing ball, they're swimming. This place can be a positive experience for you. You'll learn Torah; you'll play sports; it'll be fun."

For the next two days I stayed to myself, dimly aware of a sensation of pulling in, as if my personality were going dormant. I rarely spoke. After dinner on my second night, my brother sat down next to me. "I don't think you're real comfortable here," he observed. My brother was not an insensitive man and seemed sincerely concerned about me.

"Izzy, if you really don't like it, you don't have to stay." He was very apologetic and quickly realized that this was shaping up to be a disaster. The next morning he put me on a bus back to Manhattan, where my sister and brother-in-law were waiting.

I had not seen much of Miriam since she had married and moved to New York several years earlier. That was fine with me, since

I had never gotten along with her. She was as ultra-Orthodox as my brother but lacked key human attributes, such as compassion, that Yaakov possessed. Miriam had doubled-down on her unpleasant personality traits by marrying Mordecai.

They met me with scowls and a command to "Get in the car." The two of them were furious with me for ruining the plan—what that plan was, exactly, no one had explained to me. On the way to their apartment I kept quiet, my mind narrowing into survival mode. I had no idea what would happen next and fastened onto the idea of getting back to Camp Moshava. I knew where the Greyhound station was now; I had some money . . . silently I plotted my escape.

My sister and brother-in-law were not as reserved. Between the two of them they could have drowned out a locomotive. They saw themselves as caretakers of the Eichenstein dynasty and guardians of righteousness, and my rejection of Camp Stone Age made them apoplectic—which was bizarre given that I was just a kid in high school.

"You are hurting this family," my brother-in-law yelled as he propelled his huge automobile through the crowded streets. "You will cooperate. I'm not your father," he warned, as if Dad were Walt Disney and I had been living it up in Fantasyland. "This behavior is over. You're going to get in line."

Never underestimate what people will do in the name of saving your soul. When we arrived at their home, my sister held out her hand. "Wallet," she said, stone-faced. I handed it over. Now I could not buy a bus ticket, but as soon as they left to go food shopping, I called the director at Camp Moshava and begged him to let me return.

"I'll see what I can do, Izzy," he promised. "I'll call your father." I never heard back from him. (Forty years later I actually got the chance to ask this man what had happened. "I called people in your family, including your sister, to try to get you back. They said, 'Izzy needs to be in a different environment. Don't call here again.'")

I stayed with my sister and her husband for three days. By then the family had a new plan for me. It was another Torah learning camp in the same area of the Catskills as Camp Stone Age, but slightly more modern.

"I do not want to go there! I want to go back to Camp Moshava," I insisted, but I knew it was pointless. My sister and her husband were so invested in the yeshivah lifestyle that any objections were viewed as blasphemous and morally wrong. It was the standard fundamentalist mind-set. As far as they were concerned, outsiders who defect may be tolerated but those who are born into the group and choose to leave are perceived as mortal threats. They must be forced back into the fold or ejected from it entirely. I had no choice but to follow my family's directives. I was fifteen years old, I had no money, and no one was in my corner. My sister and her husband dropped me off at Port Authority and I took what was becoming a familiar trip back to Monticello, where a counselor from the camp met me.

I arrived at Camp Morris—my third camp in ten days—numb and disoriented.

Morris was considered the premier yeshivah camp on the East Coast and had more amenities than Camp Stone Age, meaning cabins in decent repair and facilities that did not appear to be health and safety hazards. As I exited the car I saw that all the boys were wearing black hats. Later I found out that the Woodstock music festival had been taking place that very weekend only fifteen minutes away. We knew nothing about it because there was a total information blackout in the yeshivah camps.

I let the counselor lead me upstairs to a small dormitory-type room. I sat on the bed, my mind a blank. There was no way out.

"Come down for dinner," the counselor called as he shut the door.

I'm not coming down for nothin', I thought, and decided to go on a hunger strike.

In this yeshivah there was a *mashgiach*, like there had been at my Jewish day school. Here it was a rabbi who acted as a guidance counselor and was in charge of helping the students assimilate, talking to them about their problems. After dinner that night, Camp Morris's mashgiach knocked on my door. He had a long beard and a long black coat. "You know, you have to eat to survive," he said, opening the door and regarding me kindly. They had chosen their mashgiach well—he was a very sweet man. Every few hours over the next two days he would knock. "Would you like to take a walk with me? We'll talk?"

"No."

On the third day I said to myself, "You know what? I'm not gonna win this battle." I was not going to stay locked in my room. I had to make peace with all of this. Going back to my summer camp in Wisconsin was off the table. I was stuck. My soul was dying but I had no choice. I went down to the dining hall . . . hey, even captives get hungry.

Other than eating meals, I kept to myself for the first ten days. There were plenty of sports, but I didn't have the juice to participate. As for the evening Torah learning sessions, they would have needed a cattle prod to get me to one of those. I stayed in my room, thinking about nothing.

About two weeks after my arrival I called my parents to say hello and that's when the next directive came down.

"You will not be returning to Yeshivah High School in Chicago for eleventh grade," my father informed me. His tone was so cold that I could barely muster a stunned, "I'm not? Where am I going?"

"Camp Morris has many students from serious yeshivahs. Maybe one of them will know of a school that will be acceptable to us and will also accept you. Call us when you have found a new school. Good-bye." He hung up.

It was almost August, and the beginning of the school year was only one month away. Besides feeling panicked, I was flooded with the fresh fear that my parents seemed to genuinely dislike me. I honestly wondered if this was what it felt like to be an orphan. Not only had my mother and father pulled me out of summer camp, they were now prohibiting me from going back to my high school or moving home with them. I was never in serious trouble in high school. I was not a bad kid, but I sure felt like one now. I remember vowing to myself that I would never reject anybody for anything because rejection felt like the most severe emotional pain a person could experience.

I started asking around about schools. What would happen to me if I didn't find someplace to go? Would I stay at Camp Morris all winter? That would be impossible, but it seemed nothing was impossible now. About a week after my father's instructions, I was sitting in the dining hall at lunch when an older boy of about nineteen turned to me and asked, "How are you doing?"

"*Baruch Hashem*, good," I replied automatically. In this camp, as in my extended family, *Baruch Hashem*—"Thank God"—preceded every comment. But instead of the usual follow-up, "What Torah portion are you studying today?" this boy asked, "So where do you learn? What yeshivah do you attend?"

"For the last two years I've been studying at a school in Chicago, but next year I don't know where I'm going."

It turned out that this student, and some others at the table, attended a new yeshivah in Pittsburgh that was an offshoot of a very respected academy in New York.

"The head of the school is coming here on Friday. Maybe you should go to our yeshivah in Pittsburgh."

Maybe I should, I thought to myself. *It's as good a place as anywhere.*

My interview with the head of school could not be described as rigorous. The fledgling institution needed students. When he heard that my name was Izzy Eichenstein, his face lit up. "I know all about your family!" I smiled politely as he gushed about how holy and wonderful they were, how important, he knew this cousin, that cousin. . . . It sounded like a commercial for the Eichenstein family.

He then gave me a perfunctory test on the Talmud, but basically he just wanted to hear that I could speak a few words of Hebrew. The interview amounted to, *You have shoes and moving parts, you seem like a nice guy, you're in.*

"Welcome, Yisroel," he said grandly, using my Hebrew name. Good-bye Izzy—I was now Yisroel. He could have called me Juan and I wouldn't have cared. I had to find someplace to go for eleventh grade.

I immediately phoned my father. "You'll never guess who I met with today."

"We'll look into this place and get back to you," he said, when I had described the encounter.

I don't know if there is a *Zagat's Guide* to Serious Yeshivot, but if so, someone in the family must have consulted it and given the new school in Pittsburgh a thumbs-up. When my parents called to tell me that it was acceptable, I felt every muscle in my body relax.

As for my parents, they could not have been happier if I had won the lottery. This was apparently a step up from my school in Chicago. I had been called up to the major leagues. Bring out the trumpets and horns, the full orchestra! Within the day, my brother and sister had phoned to congratulate me, and I even received calls from my morally crusading cousins, Velvel and Rabbi Naftali.

It felt good. Finally, a breakthrough. When I returned home from Camp Morris, there were no more icy looks from my parents or the extended family. Instead, I was treated to warmth, hugs, and acceptance. To prepare for my new life and persona, I had to dress the part. Off went the blue jeans, the T-shirt, the longish hair. On went the black hat, the black suit, and a crew cut. The black hat is the ticket in the ultra-Orthodox world; it is your shiny new Corvette. Like a Chasidic Platinum American Express Card, the black hat opens doors. I told myself I was ready to walk through them.

~~~

I arrived in Pittsburgh with my short hair and black hat, resolved to make my parents and the family proud. I was going to study non-stop. I was going to be a straight-A student. All my life, for as long as I could remember, I had felt as if there were something in my genetic makeup that repelled my family. I hated the feeling that they didn't like me and I knew it wasn't my imagination. I didn't fit in. I didn't belong. That September I was convinced that it was now or never—I would be the person they wanted. I studied relentlessly, and although I still had a terribly difficult time concentrating, through sheer determination I started getting As. The fact that we weren't allowed to read newspapers, watch television, go to the movies, see girls, or listen to music on the radio, cut down on the distractions. If you were caught going to a movie, you were suspended.

My dorm was a converted apartment building on Bartlett Street. It was two doors away from a twenty-four-hour gas station. I remember straining my ears at the window, trying to hear the music coming from the mechanics' transistor radio. Thank goodness they enjoyed blasting it— at least I could hear fragments of my favorite songs. I used to take long walks by myself so I could catch strains of music or sports scores from passing cars.

The head rabbi, who had recruited me, soon saw that I had a much less rigidly Orthodox background than the other students, most of whom were from Brooklyn and had grown up in the black-hat environment. He tried his best, in his own way, to keep me from losing my mind—not by having long talks with me about Torah but by leaving me alone. He was a good and honorable man. He looked the other way when my inherent "rebelliousness" surfaced, this time taking the form of sneaking over on the occasional Saturday to join a modern Orthodox youth group similar to one I had belonged to in Chicago, B'nai Akiva. I met a girl there and we became friends, almost boyfriend and girlfriend. Students at my yeshivah were allowed to accept weekend invitations to Shabbat meals at the homes of various families, and I managed to be invited over to this house, repeatedly, so I was able to develop a relationship with the daughter. It provided me with a little relaxation and a place to be more like the boy I used to be. The head of the school could have disciplined me for visiting this family's house because it wasn't within the yeshivah mandate to go visit a girl. Instead, he left me alone. It was a generous act that I interpreted as his having respect for me. I think he felt bad for me. Many years later, he spoke with my wife and intimated that he blamed the family for the terrible treatment I had endured up until that point.

Although I was generally in the family's good graces now, every now and then I'd get a reminder of the bad old days. At one family function I attended while living in Pittsburgh, an ultra-Orthodox rabbi asked me what I was studying that day. Since it was the anniversary of the founding of the State of Israel I replied, "I'm reciting prayers thanking God for the creation of the State of Israel." He slapped me across the face. Why? Because many ultra-Orthodox Jews reject the State of Israel on the grounds that it is not religiously based. I didn't know that. Getting slapped in the face definitely burned it into my memory.

I got straight As in all my classes both my junior and senior years. When I took breaks during the Jewish holidays and visited relatives in New York, they lavished me with praise: "We're hearing such wonderful things about you, how you're learning Torah, becoming a scholar. And look at you!" Delighted, they would take in my black suit, black hat, and short-cropped hair, all the while smiling and nodding and patting me on the back. The only thing missing was a Chasidic marching band.

The compliments and approval blew through me like a dry breeze. Detached, I barely heard their voices. All the happy feedback was not changing the way I felt. The family didn't know that I had nothing in common with my fellow yeshivah students in Pittsburgh. I tried to develop friendships with a few of my classmates, but I sensed that I could not be myself with them; I couldn't be real. They took their Judaism to a different level. Their elevator stopped at a different floor than mine. Outwardly I fit in, but to keep up the façade, I had to split Izzy off from Yisroel and relocate him somewhere in the back of my soul.

I began to draw inward. I had never been shy, but I started spending a good deal of time alone thinking and reflecting, my own version of meditation. I took many long, solitary walks around the Squirrel Hill section of Pittsburgh, which had the most beautiful trees I had ever seen. Standing under the boughs of a fiery crimson maple and staring up through the leaves, I could forget myself and float upward toward heaven.

Shortly before the end of my senior year, my brother Yaakov introduced me to his mentor. "I want you to meet the rabbi who has influenced me most to be the person I am today." The elderly rabbi, a very sweet man, came in, sat down, and proceeded to spend about thirty minutes warning me not to go to the movies. "You know why movies are bad for you, besides all the schmutz and dirt? Movies stay with you. Torah needs to stay with you, not movies." I just nodded quietly and let him talk. For the umpteenth time I asked myself, *"Is this really happening or is it just a bad dream?"* Evidently, my family thought I still needed a lot of work.

I finished high school with honors and was asked to speak at our graduation. My mother was pleased; in fact, she was glowing. My dad rewarded my two-year marathon of intensive, ultra-Orthodox training with, "Yes, you have done well. But this is a small yeshivah."

One of my teachers, who was also a professor at the University of Pittsburgh, was more effusive. "Yisroel, with your academic record I can get you into any college." It's a shame I didn't take him up on it. But I was lost and depressed and I had no idea what to do with myself. Fortunately, I was able to sidestep the dilemma. Then as now, when a student graduates from high school in the Orthodox world, the next stop is Israel.

CHAPTER 5

NEXT STOP:
THE HOLY LAND TOUR

D uring the two years I was in Pittsburgh I stayed in contact with my core friends in Chicago, including Stevie of the *Playboy* escapade and several other guys from my old group. Some of the kids at Camp Moshava, who had watched me drive away that summer, had kept in touch too. All were graduating from high school, and many were planning to go to Israel for at least one year. Most of them would be spending that time studying in a modern Orthodox yeshivah or living on a religious *kibbutz* (commune).

Unlike many of the *kibbutzim* in the 1970s which were secular, religious kibbutzim combined studying Torah with agricultural work in a communal environment with other religious families. This model was Orthodox, but it was quite different from the ultra-Orthodox lifestyle of my family. Religious laws were taken very seriously, however; the students dressed casually (no black hats here) and they even wore sandals without socks (unthinkable in the ultra-Orthodox world!). Dating girls was still considered to be preparation for matrimony, but among my group, lots of guys had girlfriends and it wasn't exactly considered a sin. So, while very religious, a religious kibbutz was not exactly a monastery.

For my former classmates, a kibbutz would mean full immersion in the religious lifestyle. For me, however, even a religious kibbutz was out of the question. My family thought it would be too "modern," not religious enough, not "black-hat" style. It didn't meet their standards. I would have to choose a much stricter environment in Israel where I would be housed in a dorm with black-hat restrictions similar to those I lived with in the Pittsburgh yeshivah.

By this time my relationship with the extended family was excellent. My personal stock had climbed to an all-time high, and the rabbis who dominated the Eichenstein clan were friendly to me. While making my plans for Israel, I decided to utilize their goodwill.

I had discovered a highly regarded yeshivah, Kerem B'Yavneh, which was located next to Kibbutz Yavneh, where some of my friends would be living. But when I tried to reserve a spot at Kerem B'Yavneh, I discovered they had all been filled. One call to a well-placed second-cousin and—shazzam!—I was accepted. Still emotionally raw from my two grueling years in the black-hat world, and still stinging from my father's "meh" assessment of my triumphs there, I gladly packed my black-and-white wardrobe and boarded the plane to Israel.

For all the talk about Israel I listened to while growing up, no one had prepared me for the awe that flooded me when I stepped onto the concourse at Lod (now Ben Gurion International) Airport. All around me I heard Hebrew. As I made my way to baggage claim, I felt like part of an epic in-gathering of the exiles. Every face spoke to me: *I am from Yemen. I am from Syria. I am the child of a Holocaust survivor. Israel is my home—I am free to be a Jew here in the land of my ancestors. My people have been chased and slaughtered all over the world, and if I wasn't here, I would probably be dead.* I felt their words in the deepest part of my soul.

A cousin was putting me up for a week before my studies at the yeshivah began, so I had seven days to tour the sites around Jerusalem. I planned on cramming in as much as I humanly could. After I unpacked my suitcase, I took out my radio and slowly dialed through the channels, still not quite believing that every single voice was speaking Hebrew. Eventually I collapsed on the bed, slept for ten hours, and woke up the next morning raring to explore the ancient city.

All the major faiths have holy connections to Jerusalem. You sense it, and you can be overcome by it. Jerusalem should have its own time zone, Holy Standard Time, for you do feel the holiness of the city when you are there. The voices of the past, and of all faiths, resonate in the air. For someone like me, who had always been extremely sensitive to the vibrations around me, the energy in Jerusalem was a constant buzz that never faded, even late at night.

On my first day as a tourist, I walked to the Western Wall, taking a route through the Old City. Entering the Arab market, I melded into the crowd of Chasidic Jews, Reform Jews, Christians, Muslims, and who knows what other seekers. A jumble of languages filled my ears, and the air was thick with the scents of grilled meat, spices, incense, animals, and humans. After a lifetime cloistered in my Orthodox world, the scene was overwhelming. At the Wall, I craned my neck to see the top layer of massive stones, but the bright sun seemed to bleach them into the sky. The atmosphere rippled with the prayers of millions of people who had made this journey before me.

The next day, I visited Yad Vashem, Israel's national Holocaust memorial. Once again I was overcome, this time by the enormity of the building and what it contained: an attempt to document in words and photographs a record of every soul taken by the Holocaust. After wandering through the memorial's vast halls and peering into cases filled with the personal possessions of the victims; after gazing at hundreds of photographs, not only of wartime atrocities but also of the families who were lost, I left the memorial in a daze.

From that solemn hall I walked out into the lively streets where a construction crew seemed to be pounding and drilling on every corner. Only four years earlier, in 1967, Jerusalem had been divided; now it was united under the flag of Israel and the city was surging.

I couldn't stop thinking about all the blood that had been spilled just to get this piece of land. At that time, the early 1970s, almost everyone in the country had been touched by the Holocaust. The sight of young Israeli soldiers walking the streets with their heads held high had a profound effect on me.

When my week of sightseeing was over, I braced myself for the yeshivah. If I didn't feel all that enthusiastic about devoting myself to school again, at least I was impressed with the State of Israel. Maybe that would be enough to jump-start me into my studies. Before I checked in at Kerem B'Yavneh, I had one more stop to make, a family-requested visit to a rabbi cousin who was the head of an ultra-Orthodox yeshivah outside of Jerusalem. A somewhat charismatic yet doctrinaire person, he had already established a large group of followers, both in Israel and around the Orthodox world. Sometimes it seemed that the Eichensteins really did have a monopoly on the earth's supply of Orthodox rabbis. (Online you can buy "Torah Personalities"— rabbi trading cards that are collected by the Orthodox faithful. I am not making this up. I would venture to guess that my family is very well represented. Except for me. I am definitely not on a trading card).

When I arrived at my cousin's house, he was sitting with what looked to be a religious businessman from America. My cousin was clearly pitching the man for a financial contribution to his yeshivah. After briefly greeting me, my cousin launched back into to his pitch. I sat quietly and watched. Finally the businessman asked,"Rabbi, what is the difference between your yeshivah and the yeshivah your cousin sitting here will be going to?"

My cousin walked over to me, put his hand on my head, and plucked up my knit yarmulke, displaying it as if it were Specimen A in a science project. "We wouldn't let him in wearing this kind of yarmulke. It would be unacceptable. We are a real yeshivah, black-hat only."

My cousin's dismissal of me, my yarmulke, and my future school was rude even by black-hat standards, so I left as quickly as possible and made my way to Yeshivah Kerem B'Yavneh.

Kerem B'Yavneh was designed to be a peaceful refuge for serious students, a place where they might develop not only a greater understanding of Torah but also a love of Israel. It was this combination of Torah learning and Zionism that I thought would save my spirit. It might be the best of both worlds. The truth, as I later realized, was that it had no appeal for me whatsoever. I was done with this life, honestly, I had nowhere else to go. The dogma of this yeshivah was as structured as any other, and I was only just starting to learn that dogma has no boundaries and holds many people captive.

The Kerem B'Yavneh campus was lovely. It sprawled over many acres and was lushly landscaped with huge palms, olives, and other native trees. The dorms were clean and comfortable; the classrooms were bright and well kept. The centerpiece of Kerem B'Yavneh was an enormous *beit midrash*, or study hall, with a magnificent barrel ceiling that reached forty feet at its height. The room was large enough for hundreds of students to study simultaneously at long rows of tables. When I peeked in, I saw a sea of white shirts and black pants. No black hats, because this was a knit yarmulke yeshivah, as my cousin had pointed out. But the students here were obviously every bit as intent on learning as their black-hatted counterparts. I would discover that no matter the time of day or night, the biet midrash was full of young men studying Torah.

On the first day of classes, all the new students were called in to the beit midrash. We were given name tags and told to stand in line, like the scene in a movie where the sergeant reviews a fresh batch of recruits. Here the sergeant was the head of school, or *rosh yeshivah*, and had been the leader of this academy for more than two decades. He slowly walked the line, ignoring most of the students but occasionally greeting someone by name. When he came to me he stopped and announced in a loud voice, "Yisroel Eichenstein. I received a phone call from your relatives. You are only here because of your family name." Then, leaning in more closely to me, he muttered, "You don't deserve to be here." Humiliated and furious, I said nothing and stared straight ahead. I should have asked, "Rabbi, why did you say yes? Did my relatives put a gun to your head?" I would have saved both of us many months of aggravation.

The rosh yeshivah's remarks rattled me badly but I still intended to immerse myself in Torah studies. As far as I could tell, most of the other students felt supremely lucky to have been accepted at Kerem B'Yavneh. They came not only from the United States but also from across Europe and South America. I could see the excitement in their eyes—they were giddy at being in this exclusive academy where they would get to sing, dance, pray, study, eat, live, sleep, and dream Torah 24/7. In classes, at meals, and on the paths and lawns of the campus, the students' voices could be heard in passionate discussion and debate. Although the facilities were spacious, we were packed in tightly together, almost shoulder to shoulder at the desks and study-hall tables. After the first week, the flush in the students' faces had not faded. Few events in life surpass one's wildest dreams, but for those students, Kerem B'Yavneh delivered.

By the beginning of the second week, I knew I was in trouble. Two years' worth of intensive study in Pittsburgh seemed to have receded to the far corners of my brain. I could not grasp the Jewish concepts. When I couldn't follow the teachers' lectures, it only reinforced what the rosh yeshivah had said: I didn't belong there. At this yeshivah, the students typically studied in partnership or *chevrusah.* Two students would sit across from each other and go over a Torah or Talmud portion, debating the various meanings and delving as deeply as possible into the text. The sessions might last several hours. My partner started out eager to work with me, but he might as well have been speaking Swahili. It was agonizing for both of us. No matter how hard I struggled, I just didn't comprehend the texts. The light had gone off. A terrifying thought flitted at the edge of my mind: rosh yeshivah's. I didn't let that idea form into a concrete sentence but it settled right near the surface of my consciousness.

The main reason I was at Kerem B'Yavneh in the first place was to have access to my friends who were living in the kibbutz next door, and during the first several weeks I visited them often. But to my dismay, I quickly saw that we were moving in opposite directions. The rigorous level of study was new to my friend Stevie and the others, and they were charged up by it. They were plugging into the religious life of Israel in a beautiful way while I was failing to connect.

During the first month of my stay at Kerem B'Yavneh, my kibbutz friends sometimes came to visit for a day or two to share meals and study with us. At mealtime, it was common for students to give a *d'var Torah*—to speak about an aspect of the week's Torah portion that had personal significance. One weekend, my friend Jeff came to stay with me. After the Saturday afternoon meal, he spoke for fifteen minutes. When he was done, he suddenly turned to me and said, "How come you never give a *d'var Torah*?"

Because I don't want to. Because I don't like this. The thoughts sprang into my head before I could push them down.

"I don't know. Don't put me on the spot," I mumbled.

It was a turning point. Now that Jeff had outed me to myself, it was as if the mist had cleared to reveal an iceberg. There was no denying that my family had been right: I was not Torah-true.

I loved being a Jew, but I could not get comfortable with this type of Judaism. I knew from the days of growing up in my dad's synagogue that there were many ways to be Jewish, to live a proud Jewish life without being held captive to the rules and having my self-esteem attacked at every step. On my days off, touring and watching through the windows of my supervised travel buses, I saw lots of happy and free people who were glad to be Jewish and were proud of their heritage yet felt good about themselves. At this point I had no secular friends and no role models—no road map. I couldn't conceive of what form my religion might take if it was not Orthodox. I was embarrassed by who I was and I felt horribly guilty. If there was a word that could sum it all up, it was *shame*. Going to class became excruciating. Nothing was penetrating my brain, and my panic and guilt were growing by the day, so I stopped going to class.

It was easy to walk out the front doors of the yeshivah, as easy as walking off any college campus. The first time I did it, a dam inside me broke. I was going to see the land and enjoy myself! Each day I roamed the city, and on weekends I took off and toured around the countryside. On my third weekend out, as I was hitchhiking in the north, I met a female soldier from Kibbutz Ginossar, one of Israel's more secular kibbutzim. She invited me to her kibbutz, where I spent a few days and met her family, who treated me like an old friend. What a breath of fresh air it was! Her parents, her whole community, were living proud Jewish lives without religious tyranny.

I returned from Ginossar flushed with excitement and happy with my new experience. I confided in one of my roommates, who was an Israeli who had already completed his army service and was in a very different place than me. He immediately reported my extracurricular activities to the rosh yeshivah. "Yisroel is not yeshivah material; he doesn't belong here." After the afternoon prayer service, the rosh yeshivah called me into his office, berated me for ten minutes, and capped off his lecture with, "Any more trouble from you and I'm kicking you out and sending you back to the States."

I forced myself to start attending classes again, at least a couple of times a week. But all my good intentions about studying had evaporated. I sat there observing the other students as they jumped to their feet to exclaim over this or that Torah reading, or stood at the lectern swaying back and forth with the intensity of their insights. There was a lot of singing and dancing after meals, at services, and at holidays. There is a lot of exuberance in yeshivot; mostly it is religious fervor, some of it is pure Chasidic joy. I was living inside an ecstatic Orthodox musical—*Yeshivah!*—but I was deaf to it. I had fallen off the path.

CHAPTER 6

REB SHLOMO'S
HOLY *HIPPELACH*

T hroughout the summer and into the fall of 1971 I continued to skip classes and wander the country. I was in a fog,
searching for any type of direction. By January 1972 I was
still enrolled in Kerem B'Yavneh but knew that eventually the rosh
yeshivah would send me packing. I didn't think about what I would
do then.

One day, I found myself in Jerusalem, wandering around and
observing life in the city. Near the King David Hotel, I saw a crowd
of young people singing and dancing, stirring up a big commotion
in the town square. I strolled over to investigate. As I got closer I saw
about fifty kids my age dressed in all kinds of colorful garb. If central casting was seeking a crowd of Jewish hippies, this would have
been it. What made the scene even more compelling to me was that
among the crowd were quite a few pretty girls. Who was it that these
young people were listening to and following so intently? As I leaned
in to hear the song, I suddenly recognized it from my youth. The one
and only Reb Shlomo Carlebach was leading this joyful group.

Composer, performer, teacher, storyteller—Shlomo Carlebach
was all of these and more. He had been raised in an ultra-Orthodox
community in Germany before World War II and had been trained
as a rabbi. However, he had chafed against the strict and severe con-

fines of ultra-Orthodox Judaism and developed his own brand of Chasidism, complete with dancing, joy, and inclusion. Shlomo Carlebach's music was hugely popular everywhere in the Jewish world, from Chasidic shtibels to Reform congregations, and young people adored him. I had grown up listening to Reb Shlomo's songs in my Jewish day schools, youth groups, and at Camp Moshava. His albums (he would eventually record twenty-five of them) were my soundtrack to Jewish life. When I was a young boy, Reb Shlomo would occasionally perform in Chicago. All the little kids would sit onstage with him—a Shlomo Carlebach concert was a happening.

It had been years since I had laid eyes on the man, but I had never spoken to him. Now he was in his mid-forties. His full, dark beard was beginning to go silver at the edges, as was his hair, which had already receded to the top of his skull. What remained of the hair curled almost to his collar. Reb Shlomo favored blue jeans and white shirts, like all good bards of that era. Warmth beamed out of him. He was a legend, a rebel, and a rock star rabbi all wrapped in one.

When the singing and dancing ended, Reb Shlomo spied me standing at the edge of the crowd. He strode over to me. "Brother, I am Shlomo. What is your name?"

"Izzy Eichenstein," I replied.

"And your Hebrew name?"

"Yisroel."

"Yisroel Eichenstein" His eyes grew wide with warmth. "You know, I went to yeshivah with your cousins. One of my first public performances was at your cousin's wedding back in the 1950s."

For once I was glad to hear about a family connection. Shlomo hugged me and said, "Welcome to Jerusalem! Come and walk with me to my apartment."

On the way there, snippets of what I knew about Shlomo Carlebach flew through my head. I recalled seeing a large color photograph of him on the back page of *Life* magazine. In it, he had flowers in his hair and was presiding over a marriage ceremony in San Francisco's Golden Gate Park. Reb Shlomo had a home there that was known as the "House of Love and Prayer." It was a place where young people who were getting into Judaism, many of them for the first time, could meet and pray with him when he was in town. Reb Shlomo spent most of the year traveling and performing. His home base was in Manhattan but he also had residences in San Francisco and Jerusalem.

The Jerusalem apartment was like an international version of the House of Love and Prayer. It was a large, welcoming space where men and women mingled together easily. The proximity of so many women was exhilarating to me after a lifetime of being in the all-male yeshivah world. But what these kids found so intoxicating about the House of Love and Prayer was the loving acceptance for who they were and whatever part of the Jewish journey they were on. Everyone was welcome to join the ride. To this day, I have yet to meet anyone as accepting and loving as Reb Shlomo Carlebach. Even ultra-Orthodox people would secretly confide in Shlomo in their darkest hours. But that was behind the scenes; they would not, at that time, be caught openly conversing with him.

I spent many all-nighters at Reb Shlomo's, seeing how he stayed up until the wee hours listening intently to people talk about their personal issues and struggles. Shlomo specialized in individuals who were lost. Even now I hate to use that word to describe myself, but it's the truth. Shlomo took lost souls, gathered them in, and made them feel at home. He was like a bridge of hope for the young people I met in Jerusalem, whom he dubbed "Holy *Hippelach*."

Shlomo was one of those rare human beings who can lift you to a better place, who have faith in who you are and—just as important—like and accept who you are. There are very few people who are able to lift your soul, and when you are in their presence, you are at peace. No inner rebellion, no internal war, just the flow of your soul at peace. That is how it felt to be with Reb Shlomo Carlebach.

In a matter of months, I accepted Reb Shlomo's offer to live at the House of Love and Prayer. The Rosh Yeshivah at Kerem B'Yavneh was thrilled to see me go. If he could have hired a parade with a marching band to lead me out, he would have. I had told Shlomo how depressed and isolated I had felt, not only in Jerusalem but also at the yeshivah in Pittsburgh. At one point, I had Shlomo phone my parents and talk to them and after a few minutes he understood my challenges. He probably worried that I might bolt out of Jerusalem altogether if he didn't offer a safe haven.

When my parents heard that I was living with Reb Shlomo, they were quite distressed. They called my cousin, the rabbi who had ridiculed my knitted yarmulke, and begged him to admit me to his black-hat yeshivah in a last-ditch effort to save my soul. I moved a suitcase into the dorms for appearance's sake and kept staying at Shlomo's. A month later I went back to collect the suitcase.

My time at the House of Love and Prayer was spent mostly going to concerts with Shlomo, singing a lot, dancing a lot, and traveling around the country with a gang of ragamuffin musicians. Shlomo gave me my first guitar and taught me my first guitar chords. Although it had a crack, it had the sweetest sound, the sound of freedom. I even performed with Shlomo onstage at several concerts, and there is still TV footage of me in his concerts available on YouTube. You can see me in a white knit yarmulke, a beard, and a white yeshivah shirt sitting near him. It was an amazing time in my life.

Although I was much happier living at the House of Love and Prayer than at my cousin's yeshivah, I didn't have a lot in common with most of the other young people there. Ninety-eight percent of them had no religious training or background, whereas I was the opposite. In fact, Shlomo asked me to help some of the kids learn Hebrew. They were drawn to Shlomo because he was a bridge into the religious world. It's a testament to how compassionate and open-minded Shlomo was that, for me, he was a bridge out of it. Shlomo identified with those who did not fit in. At that time he himself was not in good standing with mainstream Orthodox Judaism. His songs were popular, but his non-Orthodox behavior and his hippie entourage were looked down upon by the Orthodox world. He did not care. Countless times he told me, "Brother, I do my thing everywhere—nightclub, synagogue, yoga institute— it doesn't matter where, I just do it." It's quite sad that the ultra-Orthodox didn't appreciate him until he passed away and then tried to claim ownership of him. But Shlomo was an original; he did his own thing. No one owned him. Shlomo Carlebach was exceptionally good to me and supported my tentative first steps outside the black-hat world. I needed someone as strong as he was to help me stand up to the family. Without Reb Shlomo, who knows how long it would have taken?

~~~

In the spring of 1972 I moved from Jerusalem to New York City. I was still on a quest to find a place where I felt at home. For a short while I attended Yeshivah University, but this was no better a fit than Kerem B'Yavneh. I soon left and enrolled instead in Teachers College, Columbia University, where I lived in the dorm. Meanwhile, I stayed in touch with Reb Shlomo who had a synagogue in New York as well as a home there. In late May, he called me into his office at the synagogue.

"Brother, you have to come to Israel with me this summer."

"But I don't have any money."

Without a moment's hesitation he wrote a check and handed it to me.

"Go get a ticket. You're coming with me."

To this day I'm not entirely sure why Shlomo was so insistent that I go with him that summer. Maybe he was concerned about me and wanted to keep an eye on me. I acted as his roadie: taking care of logistics, carrying equipment, making reservations, and doing general gofer work as we traveled around Israel. Gradually, Shlomo started giving me more responsibilities. When I came back to New York in the fall, I continued to see a lot of him. It was the start of a long working relationship that eventually led to my becoming his manager and booking his concerts all over the world.

Shlomo may have been a rabbi, but he was unlike any rabbi I had known. While so many others seemed to be all about judgment, he was all about loving other people. He famously said on many occasions, "My hope is to hug every Jew in the world." This man embraced and accepted everyone. Being around him gave me a new perspective. For the first time, I clearly understood how much my self-worth and happiness had hinged on my family's acceptance or rejection of me. Even in Pittsburgh, as I was basking in the praise and approval of the extended family, I knew that it would all be snatched away the minute I dropped the Torah-true persona and let my real self out. I was now twenty-two and could not remember a time when the threat of complete rejection had not been hanging over me. Meanwhile, this internationally beloved rabbi and musician not only accepted me, he also liked me, respected me, and even trusted me with some of his professional decisions. I felt like a creature who had been living his entire life underground and finally emerged into the daylight.

Although I was attending Columbia, I now spent the majority of my week with Shlomo and his inner circle. It was a time of discovery on every level—my own personal enlightenment. I was determined to find out what the non-Orthodox world was like. To my amazement, it was easy to converse with "regular" men and women—the ones I had always been warned were unholy, *apikorsim*, "not like us." People who have never lived in a closed community might find it hard to comprehend how shut off I had been from the rest of society, but here's one good example: It was 1972 and I had only vaguely heard of Bob Dylan.

It was while hanging out at Reb Shlomo's place that I first encountered Dylan's music. One evening, a friend called me with an invitation: "Hey, Iz, I have tickets to a Bob Dylan concert. Want to come?" I had never been to a rock concert and had no idea that Dylan was already world famous. I invited Reb Shlomo to come with us. The arena seated 15,000 people and it was packed when we got there. The lights were still on and many people recognized Shlomo. That concert opened my eyes to another world. The music, the energy, the feeling of liberation, and the depth of the music that I was hearing for the first time—it was my Passover.

Bob Dylan's music had the same life-altering effect on me that it had on millions of other people when they had first heard "Blowing in the Wind" ten years earlier. Some of Dylan's songs were spiritual, and they spoke to me on levels I had never experienced in synagogue. I must have listened to "Mr. Tambourine Man" a hundred times. It was as if those songs grabbed me and pulled me out of the dusty broom closet where my mind had been stuck. There was a world of creativity out there, a wide world of ideas besides the ones in the Bible.

After going to his concert and then listening to Dylan's songs, a surge of energy swept over me. It was so powerful that I decided I had to meet this Bob Dylan. Who was he? Was he as famous as my cousin, the Chief Rabbi of St. Louis? I reasoned that Shlomo Carlebach was a musician and Bob Dylan was a musician—maybe they would like to meet each other.

"Shlomo, you've played at all those folk festivals. Did you ever meet Bob Dylan?"

"No, but I'd love to meet Brother Bob."

"Great! I'll arrange it."

When I told people that I was going to meet with Bob Dylan, they looked at me as if I had lost my marbles. Dylan was the voice of the counterculture, revered the world over, a god of the music scene in the 1960s and 1970s. Everyone knew he was prickly, reclusive, and intimidating. I was too naïve to worry about those rumors.

A few weeks later, I read in the *New York Post* that Dylan was in New York, spending time at his Greenwich Village townhouse.

I went down to the Village, talked to people in folk clubs, and asked if they knew where Dylan lived. Finally someone tipped me off that he lived on MacDougal Street near a camera store. I found the store, and the owner told me, "Yeah, Dylan lives across the street." He pointed to a beautiful red brick townhouse. There were six apartments in the building, so I wrote on six pieces of paper, "Bob, Rabbi Shlomo Carlebach would like to meet with you," and I included my phone number. I slipped a note into each of the townhouse's six mailboxes.

A few days later the phone rang.

"This is Bob."

He knew who Shlomo Carlebach was, he said, and would definitely like to meet him. I set it up for the following week. But five minutes before Dylan's limo pulled up to Shlomo's apartment, Reb Shlomo was called away on an emergency counseling session with a newlywed couple. Dylan was gracious about the sudden change in plans. I introduced myself as Izzy Eichenstein and told him that I didn't know much about him. He looked skeptical, then dumbfounded when he saw that I was telling the truth.

"What's your Hebrew name?" Bob wanted to know.

"Yisroel."

"I'm going to call you Yisro," he decided.

Bob liked me, and that afternoon was the first of numerous meetings between us. At the time, he was grappling with his own spiritual identity. My background intrigued him and, due to my years of Torah study, I was able to hold my own during our discussions, most of which related to philosophy. He gave me a book by Proust and I gave him a copy of Rabbi Joseph Soloveitchik's *Halakhic Man*, the landmark philosophical work about living a life of religious observance. Bob had occasionally expressed interest in the Jewish Defense League, although he had never been a big supporter. I took a dim view of the JDL's single-minded, aggressive hostility toward anyone they perceived to be anti-Jewish. I pointed out that the JDL lacked an essential Jewish attribute, compassion. Who knows what Bob thought about that—he was not a big talker. He was a listener; he wanted to hear my story. We spent many evenings hanging out in the Village, drinking wine at different bar counters. I drank my first burgundy with him. I don't remember a lot about those conversations but I know that we talked into the wee hours of the morning.

Bob had visited Israel four times in the previous two years. He and his wife, Sara, had toured the Old City of Jerusalem and the yeshivah at Mount Zion. "The difference between me and you, Yisro, is simple," he said. "You have roots. I don't." The former Bob Zimmerman had plenty of roots in Judaism, but a few years after our meetings, he decided they didn't apply to him. He became a born-again Christian. During one phone call he told me that he was praying for me.

Bob and I stayed in touch through the mid-1980s. He was always friendly and generous and would leave concert tickets for me whenever he was in town. He and Reb Shlomo never did meet, which is a shame. I would have loved to witness that conversation.

Bob Dylan and Rabbi Shlomo Carlebach both seemed tuned in to otherworldly channels. Both men's music was profound and prayerful; their songs touched millions of people in the deepest part of their being. More than any other art from, music is a path into the soul. Rabbi Shneur Zalman of Lyiady famously said that while words may be the pen of the heart, song is the pen of the soul. Words and melodies, in the right combination, can lift you, inspire you, change you, and even mold you. The original Chasidim knew this. They believed that the heartbeat of life is holy joy and that one of the best ways to express it is through music. In the 1700s, when the first Chasidic Jews rebelled against the dry, orderly style of traditional Jewish worship, they made music a cornerstone of their religious services and holidays.

One of the more ironic aspects of my upbringing was that despite being the offspring of two important Chasidic families, I knew very little about the roots of Chasidism. My father and I never discussed it. It never occurred to me to ask about the Baal Shem Tov, founder of Chasidism, or to research his life. Now I began to wonder about this man who changed the course of Judaism a little over 200 years ago. What did he represent and how did I connect to him? According to family history, I was a direct descendant of this spiritual seeker.

Delving into the life of the Baal Shem Tov, I learned that he spent much time meditating in the forests. There, he communed with nature in his quest to recreate Judaism in a fresh way. He believed that "the simple blessing of the unlettered Jew was as holy as advanced Torah study; purity of intent was valued over dry achievement; joy and humility were to be admired; and even the simplest peasant could serve G-d through passionate prayer."[2]

One legend about the Baal Shem Tov reminded me of Reb Shlomo's desire to "hug every Jew on earth." The story goes that the father of the Baal Shem Tov, who was a rabbi, died when the boy was five years old. His last words to his son were,

"Fear nothing but G-d alone. Love every single Jew, without exception, with the full depth of your heart and with the fire of your soul, no matter who he is or how he behaves." Reb Shlomo's attitude of loving acceptance closely mirrored the spirit of the Baal Shem Tov.

When the Chasidic movement began, the teachings of the Baal Shem Tov were vilified by Orthodox rabbis. The religious leaders were suspicious of the Baal Shem Tov's mystical leanings and his insistence that God could be found even in mundane activities carried out by lowly peasants. The rabbis claimed that the Baal Shem Tov was angling to be seen as a messiah. They rejected him and banned his doctrine. I could only imagine the courage it took to strike out against the rigid dogma of the religious leaders of the day.

---

2. Habad.org:
http://www.chabad.org/library/article_cdo/aid/1208507/jewish/Biography.htm

Song and dance were at the heart of the Chasidic movement, which taught that God exists in all of us and that music is one way Jews can express their joy in God. At the Jewish day schools and youth groups I attended, we would sing and dance to the music of Shlomo Carlebach. Many of his songs were prayers set to hauntingly lovely melodies. They were as familiar to me as "Twist and Shout" was to other kids in the 1960s. When I got to know Shlomo and later learned about the history of the Baal Shem Tov, a part of my legacy finally made sense to me. The spirit of acceptance was a core part of my heritage.

Reb Shlomo Carlebach was an extraordinary composer and performer. He could inspire any group to get up and dance, from a non-Jewish audience in Germany to non-religious Jews who began the concert seemingly stapled to their chairs and ended it clapping, singing, and shaking like a crowd of teenagers. I was with Shlomo when he taught and performed at yoga festivals and non-Jewish spiritual retreats, and he never failed to lift the group through his songs, his beautiful Chasidic teachings, and his aura, which was quite powerful. In those days, Shlomo liked to have young people come up on stage to sing with him. I often joined him for a song or two—my guitar skills were very basic, but I wasn't shy, so up I'd climb up to share the limelight and the joy for a little while.

I spent three years in New York City working as Shlomo's roadie, manager, and occasional side man and attending Teachers College part-time. My student status secured me a dorm at Columbia but the coursework didn't click for me. My real education was internal, a slow and painful progression away from orthodoxy.

If my sister and her husband had not lived in the city, or if I could have limited my visits to them, my overall experience in New York might have gone a little more smoothly. But Miriam and Mordecai's apartment was only ten minutes from Columbia University. I kept going there looking for love and approval that never did come.

Miriam tried to be nice to me but she just couldn't make herself do it. My "bad boy" ways and my association with Bob Dylan confounded her, although she didn't really believe me when I told her I was spending time with him. Miriam was especially incensed that the trappings of her brand of Orthodox Judaism now held zero interest for me. I wanted to keep nothing—not kosher, not religious holidays, nothing. It only validated her assessment that Reb Shlomo was a very poor role model and that I was a ruined Jew and an embarrassment to the family. I was only twenty-two.

One Friday night I was invited to my sister's for Shabbat dinner. I showed up wearing a white turtleneck shirt instead of the expected uniform: white shirt and tie. Maybe my hair was a little longer than they liked. The yeshivah look was phasing out. My brother-in-law glared at me and they barely spoke to me that night. As I left their apartment, I felt ill. Instead of walking home, I found myself entering the subway station. It wasn't a conscious decision; my feet were leading me down the stairs. I was shaking from fear at what I was about to do. I was about to violate Shabbat by riding on a subway. I was convinced I would die by the end of the night. My anxiety only eased a bit when I woke up the next morning. But something had irrevocably changed; there would be no going back.

Because I was attending Columbia University and booking gigs for Shlomo, I was gradually branching out into the non-Jewish world. But every step in that direction was like pulling my feet out of tar. My increasing anxiety about all the changes I was making took a toll on my health. I lost my appetite and dropped to about 140 pounds. Then, in June of 1975, I came down with infectious mononucleosis. My money was running out, my education was more of a cover story than anything else, and my body felt like it had been slammed by a semi. I lay in my dorm bed for about a week before giving in and calling my parents. My time in New York came to an end.

CHAPTER 7

NOTHIN' TO LOSE

I ended up in the place I least wanted to be: my old bedroom in my parents' house in Chicago. Within one week of getting mono, I had grown so ill that I had no choice but to go home to recuperate. I arrived so weak I could barely climb the stairs. My head throbbed and I spent most of my time sleeping and wanting to be left alone. Every few hours the scent of home would seep into my subconscious and wake me up. *No, no, no . . . .* The depression I carried with me from New York would loom up like thunderheads and I'd roll over and dive back into sleep.

Being at home had only one very excellent upside: my mother. They say chicken soup is Jewish penicillin and all of Mom's cooking had those magical healing properties. As the baby of the family, I had always basked in my mother's attention and now it felt especially golden. Mom treated me with great tenderness but also with a certain caution. She was concerned about me. She wanted me to be well. She loved me with all her heart, but she and my father didn't know what to do with me. They didn't know what to do with me at ten, and they didn't know what to do with me at twenty-two.

When I was growing up, my mother would ask me every morning before she made breakfast, "Are you done *davening*?" On this visit, as soon as I was well enough to come down for breakfast, she would ask the same question. I would say yes even though I had no prayer practice anymore. I didn't want to disappoint her. I knew she was not happy with my low level of observance, which she knew about from my sister's weekly reports. But there was no point in rocking the boat while I was living in her house and eating her food.

My father became a lot nicer when I was sick. He appeared to be sincerely trying to understand me. One time, he walked into my room and heard me listening to Joan Baez. "Wow, she's terrific," he said. I was stunned. Orthodox men are forbidden to listen to the sound of a female singing. Either Dad felt sorry for me or he felt guilty about his part in my lifelong anguish and identity crisis. As I said, he was trying.

A few years earlier, when I was living in Israel, my father had brought up the subject of psychotherapy. He wasn't insinuating that I was crazy to not be going along with the ultra-Orthodox program; he was just worried about my mental state. I was never involved in drugs, but he couldn't get a handle on why I was so confused and depressed, so he urged me, "If you need to talk to somebody, I think that's a great idea."

I never took him seriously. If I went to an Orthodox therapist, I wouldn't trust him. How could his advice not be based in religion? But if I went to a therapist who was not Orthodox, he wouldn't understand what I was going through. So therapy was out of the question.

While I was recovering from mono, Dad confessed that if he had not been *forced*—that was his word—to become a rabbi, he would have been a psychotherapist. It didn't surprise me, because he was very tolerant and compassionate toward his congregants. But it was more than a little ironic. Rabbi Dad would get angry at the oddest moments and lash out at me because I wasn't religious, yet psychotherapist Dad felt very badly about what Rabbi Dad was putting me through.

As I regained my health, I was able to tune in to some of the energy vibrating around the house. My brother and sister were both married and I could see the speculation in my parents' eyes: "Maybe all Izzy needs is the right girl." I decided to nip that plan in the bud.

"Dad, please don't take this the wrong way but don't fix me up like you did with my brother and sister, like in *Fiddler on the Roof.* I'll take care of meeting women on my own time."

Dad laughed out loud at that, and he never tried to play match-maker. There was a part of my father that got a real kick out of me and it's a shame he couldn't be open to who I was. But religion was like an electric fence that separated us. If I touched it I'd get shocked, and it was hard to figure out exactly where the fence was at any given time. One day Dad would gush over Joan Baez. The next, he would scold me bitterly for not being somber enough on Tisha B'Av. There was no way to predict his moods and it was impossible for me to shrug them off.

Thanks to my mother's cooking and care, I recovered from mono in six weeks. I was back at full physical strength but my mental state was uneven. My parents' house was so imbued with strict Orthodox laws that I could almost hear the walls murmuring, "Did you say your morning prayers today? Did you say the blessings over the food?"

Now that I was healthy, the surrounding neighborhood came into sharper focus. Like a Chasidic *Brigadoon*, it never changed. Within a few miles was my father's synagogue; the synagogue of my cousin, the head Chasidic Rebbe of Chicago; the apartment of my grandmother, the Rebbitzin, who held services in her living room; and my brother Yaakov's shtibl, where congregants gathered daily to study Torah. If I had wanted, I could have had my choice of twelve Eichenstein-hosted prayer services every day.

Yaakov had moved back to Chicago a few years earlier and founded an ultra-Orthodox shtibl of his own. He was a hurricane when it came to religion and that influenced my mother and father. My parents were beginning to ease into retirement at about the same time Yaakov arrived. My father's congregation was aging; the men and women whom he had mentored through their child-rearing years were getting older, and many had moved out of the area to be near their grown children and grandchildren. The synagogue membership was declining, and as it did, the clock was slowing down for my dad. Yaakov was coming into his own, and he pushed my mother and father to the conservative right.

My parents were extremely observant of Jewish law, but their home was not technically Chasidic. My father did not have long side curls, but he did have a beard and my mother covered her hair. I was startled to see that when she knew Yaakov was coming over, she put on a wig. One Thanksgiving day, he told my mother that he would not join us for dinner if she made turkey because Thanksgiving was not a Jewish holiday. Mom solved that problem by cooking a chicken for Yaakov and a turkey for the rest of us. My brother didn't inherit my mother's sense of humor or her tolerant nature. He refused to step foot inside my father's synagogue during services—the environment was treife to him. Remembering how the teenaged Yaakov had reacted when he saw Mom shake a man's hand, I figured it was best for everyone if he stayed away.

The first few weeks I was well again, I kept to myself, stayed in my room, and tried not to panic. I had no contacts in Chicago anymore; my high school friends had gone off to college or were living in Israel. I had no money, nowhere to go, and no idea what to do next.

Somehow, through the darkness, a name popped into my head: Rita Lipman. Rita was a red-haired girl who had lived a few blocks away while I was growing up. When I was in eighth grade and she was in seventh, we had belonged to the same Zionist youth group, B'nei Akiva. We used to walk home from meetings together, but when I got within a few blocks of my house, I would wander across the street or take a different route than Rita. I was afraid my family would see me with a girl and that was not appropriate.

I found Rita's number through a mutual acquaintance who told me that she was enrolled at Northwestern University in nearby Evanston. I wasted no time in calling her.

"Rita? It's Izzy. Izzy Eichenstein."

"Izzy!" She sounded pleased to hear from me. I wondered if her friend had warned her I that would be calling but I soon learned that Rita was naturally warm and gracious. "I'd love to get together," she said when I suggested a date.

A few days later we met at her apartment. It was July, and Rita was sitting outside on the steps. I'm sure she noticed my shocked grin as I tried to reconcile the Rita I remembered with this woman. Her hair was a soft, shining copper that fell in waves to just below her shoulders. Her face was classically beautiful—the cheekbones, the cover girl smile—but the lively glint in her eyes reflected more than good looks. Twelve-year-old Rita had been a nice girl. Twenty-one-year-old Rita was stunning.

I sat down next to her and we talked. Within a half hour I got the sense that this woman was different. By the end of the afternoon I had figured out why: Rita was curious about everything. She delighted in probing into all areas of a topic—religious, philosophical, psychological. I had never met a woman who asked so many questions, listened so intently to the answers, and had such provocative insights of her own. On top of it all, we had the same sense of humor—we laughed a lot on that first date. After a while we moved from her steps to my car, and then we drove around aimlessly in the long summer twilight. Many hours had passed when we finally said good night.

The next weekend I took Rita out on our first real date. We went to a place called Amazingrace in the basement of a building on the Northwestern University campus. Part coffeehouse, part commune, it was a hippie music joint masquerading as a student organization. A local musician named Bill Quateman was rocking the place—it was sweltering and ear-splitting and we stayed until closing. The temperature was in the 70s when we drove back to the city after midnight. We slowly cruised down Sheridan Road, gazing at the ghostly suburban homes and still buzzing from the music.

On that date and others that followed, Rita and I talked about everything, including our parents. Her Modern Orthodox branch of Judaism was almost as strict as my family's ultra-Orthodox branch. Rita knew all about my background. She seemed to get who I was, and I got who she was. Her parents were Holocaust survivors. Her mother had been in Auschwitz, and her father, a yeshivah student in Poland during World War II, was one of a group of Jews who had escaped to China. Her mother and father eventually relocated to Chicago where they met and married. Both were extremely devout. In another example of the close-knit community of immigrant Orthodox Jews, we discovered that the person who sponsored her father to immigrate to the United States, specifically Chicago, was none other than my Uncle Avrohom.

Rita and I instantly felt a spark that was physical, but we also felt something much deeper. She didn't feel at ease in her Orthodox world and I had never fit into mine. As our relationship grew serious, we came to an unspoken agreement: "We're going to do this our way." We wanted out. We wanted to explore life to the fullest. Rita and I were like two people jumping from an airplane with a single parachute.

In both of our families, as far as we knew, we were the *only* people of our generation who had ventured outside the Orthodox community. Everyone else went to religious school, remained devout, married Orthodox Jews, raised Orthodox children, and traveled repeatedly to Israel. Some lived there for a few years; some are still living in Israel today, thirty years later. We felt as if we were the only two who left the fold. We were each other's lifeline.

〜〜〜

Falling in love with Rita was the bridge to the next chapter of my life. Shlomo Carlebach had been the first bridge—scary for me, but a known quantity, solid and relatively safe. The relationship with Rita felt more like stepping onto a rickety suspension bridge stretched across a ravine. I knew I had to move on to the next phase, where I would truly break away, but I was scared. It felt as if a single step in the wrong direction would send me plunging to my doom.

As the weeks passed, I grew more tormented. Rita was chafing against the bonds of tradition, too, but her family was not woven into Chasidic history the way mine was. Whatever decision she made about religion, it would not reverberate much farther than her parents. My situation was more dire. I dreaded the family's reaction if I dropped the last pretense of being a devout Orthodox Jew. Worse, I was overwhelmed by fears about what would happen if I actually removed myself from that life. In the extremely structured environment in which I was raised, everything had been planned out for me since birth: the clothes I wore, the food I ate, the prayers I said, the schools I attended. If I left, I'd be cut loose from the habits and thought patterns of a lifetime. I'd be like the guy in the opening credits of *Vertigo*, spiraling down inside a bottomless vortex. What would happen to me? Who would I be? I was terrified at the prospect of having to invent a new self and carve out my own future. Rita could see how unnerved I was and she had a suggestion.

"There's this therapist . . .

"A therapist isn't going to get it, Rita."

"This one will. He used to be a rabbi. He grew up going to an Orthodox yeshivah, but now he counsels people like you."

Years later, I would learn that Israel has hotlines for Jews who want to break away from Chasidic or ultra-religious homes. There are support networks and counselors who meet privately with the defectors to guide them so they won't fall into alcohol or hard drugs. Those are very real dangers for anyone who dares to leave a closed community, be it Amish, Krishna, Scientology, Mormon, Islamic, or any group that demands absolute obedience. You're vulnerable when you leave. There's a tremendous amount of guilt and shame. I already knew how sickening it felt to be the one person in the room different from everybody else, and that was before declaring it out loud, which is what I would eventually have to do. If this therapist came from the Orthodox world, at least he would understand its rules and culture. He'd know what I was up against and maybe I could trust his perspective on my life.

"I'll try him," I promised Rita.

I didn't hold out a lot of hope as I knocked on the door of the therapist's office, but I was curious. The man who greeted me was a little overweight, jolly, and seemed extremely confident. As we introduced ourselves, I got the impression that this former rabbi was content with the choices he had made. To my surprise, within the first fifteen minutes he explained those choices.

"Let me tell you about myself. I'm now a psychologist but when I was a rabbi, I weighed nearly 300 pounds. I had an affair with the sisterhood president. I ended up leaving the rabbinate and deciding that I wanted to have a different kind of life. I don't believe in this religious stuff whatsoever." He said it with conviction. He meant it. I just stared at him, speechless.

All my life I had felt as if the real me was a second-rate version of the Torah-true person I should have been. That was the nauseating secret that had dragged me down and demoralized me. I knew I would never be at peace as long as that secret was inside me. This therapist was the first person I had met who had intentionally stepped out of the Orthodox world, and here he was announcing it as if it were perfectly normal. There was not a hint of doubt in the man.

From that point on, I saw him once a week. The sessions were a safe zone where I could be as free as he was. I told him how I had wanted to be loved and accepted by my family and to be a real part of them, but that I could not be myself within their framework. "I'm not a rebel. I want to belong, but I can't."

"You don't love that life, you love the Cubs," he said with clarity. "You've just got to acknowledge it and make peace with it. You're very spiritual but you're not into the ultra-Orthodox version of spirituality." After all those years of being bombarded with religious propaganda, it was very hard to hear but it was the truth. It was painful because it meant that I had no choice: I had to follow my heart.

The therapist's attitude was, "I know what I'm talking about and I'm never wrong." It may seem like an odd approach but for this type of counseling, it was crucial. I needed his certainty, his thick skin, his giant ego, his ability not to care what others thought and to like me for who I was. Like Shlomo, he supported me enough to help me pull away from the bullying Black Hats in my family. But whereas Shlomo was a peacemaker, this man did not shy away from a fight. Shlomo soothed my soul. Therapy showed me how to reclaim it.

In one of our early sessions, the therapist told me, "If you live your life thinking that your family is right, you'll never be happy. You have to make a decision. Do you want to live your life their way or do you want to figure out how to live it your way?"

"My way," I said without hesitation.

"You say you don't want to live in your parents' house," he continued. "Maybe you want to get a job." We sat on the floor of his office and looked at the classified ads in the *Chicago Tribune*. There was a radio station hiring someone to sell air time to advertisers. I applied for it and they called to set up an interview.

It was my first job interview out in the real world but that didn't faze me. The fact was, no one in regular society—not even Bob Dylan—intimidated me. The Black Hats had so traumatized me that everyone else seemed benevolent in comparison. Whenever I was among non-Orthodox people, it was as if an eighty-pound suitcase had been lifted from my back. I was myself: relaxed and chatty. And I was a good listener, very attuned to the other person's mood.

That's how it went at the job interview. They liked me, and I started working right away. My job had two parts: selling air time and writing ads. I learned quickly and the whole enterprise seemed almost too easy. Not that I didn't put a lot of time and effort into the work; I did. But the environment was so straightforward, the process so free from complications and anxiety, that it felt more like a game than a job.

Good-bye, old world! At twenty-two, I said hello to normal people with their own issues that had nothing to do with my background. When I walked into the radio station, the woman at reception smiled and said, "Good morning, Izzy." There were no bad vibes, Torah questions, disappointed glares, or reminders about family duty. Just, "Good morning." Then I'd go into my office and write ads or call prospects, who usually seemed happy to speak with me.

I felt so invigorated by this freedom that I quickly became the top-selling ad sales person in the country at this firm—I was earning double what the number-two salesperson was making. The world was quickly becoming my oyster (not exactly a kosher one at that), and I enjoyed every minute of this new life.

I had lived on my own and with Reb Shlomo for the two years I was in New York, but those years were nothing like this. Although it had been a time of great personal discovery, I still wrestled with Judaism every waking moment. I had not accepted myself, and as a result I was often depressed. I couldn't find a circle of people to connect with. Many of Shlomo's group were new converts to Orthodox Judaism and I didn't fit in with them any better than I did with my family. My self-esteem had been at rock bottom; I lost my appetite and my weight dropped, which probably affected my ability to fight mono.

At the radio station, I had full-out success for the first time. In Pittsburgh I had forced myself to study and I excelled, but that scholastic success had been driven by fear. If I didn't do well, I would be as good as dead to my family. In contrast, writing and selling radio ads came naturally to me. It felt right, and I was rewarded for my efforts. Within a few months, I went from having no money to making $600 or $700 a week—about $3,000 a week in 2012 dollars. Self-esteem can come from a lot of places but making money doesn't hurt.

I grew my hair long and started listening to Bruce Springsteen. At night Rita and I hit the town, checking out clubs, drinking wine, trying out cool restaurants, or just riding our bikes along Lake Shore Drive. I got my first car—a Mazda RX4 with racing stripes—and drove around Chicago thinking, *I've got the world by the tail!*

A few months after I started working at the radio station, I moved out of my parents' house and into Rita's apartment in Evanston. Naturally, we did not tell our parents about this arrangement. Soon thereafter, I decided I needed a break from my mother and father. I had not yet introduced them to Rita because I wasn't interested in having them in our lives at that time. Now I told them that I was in therapy and was not going to be contacting them for a while. For four or five months we didn't speak. My mom would phone the therapist and ask, "How come my son doesn't call me?" Of course, he couldn't and wouldn't say anything about it.

Meanwhile, I woke up every morning in Evanston with my beautiful red-headed girlfriend. It was truly a new day and I had to find out who the heck I was. Where did I want to go? What did I want to dream about and achieve? Growing up the way Rita and I had, it was incredibly difficult to develop our own passion or create something original. Everything had been so scripted for us that, at first, we devoted most of our energy to learning how to survive.

One of Dylan's lines often floated through my head that year: "When you've got nothing, you've got nothing to lose." When I arrived at my parents' house in Chicago, I had nothing and felt like nothing. Within six months, I met Rita and everything came together. It was as if a guardian angel had decreed, "This kid's been through enough. He's a good boy at heart. Let's show him how tremendous this world can be." Whoever was watching over me (maybe it was Zaide?) led Rita and me to each other. I'm absolutely sure of it. If someone asked me, "What's the proof that there's a God?" My answer would be, "Rita ended up in my life." All the other blessings flowed from that one.

The author and Israeli judge Hadassa Ben Itto, Rita's cousin.

e author's parents, Rabbi Moses Eichenstein and bbetzin Sarah Eichenstein

The author with his French cousin,
Muriel Bouhnik

Rita Fick, portraits's tegerah ceremine

The author's French cousin's extended family, with whom he had a reunion after finding them in Paris years after the war.

Shlomo Carlebach, on the left—teacher, performer, storyteller, spiritual leader, and a great friend of the author—with Rita Eichenstein and folk singer Bob Gibson

Shlomo Carlebach with the author

The author and his new bride on their wedding day

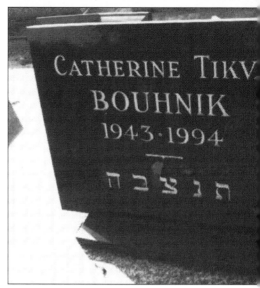

The gravesite of Catherine Tikva Bouhnik, the daughter of Tova Perlow

The author with Elli Wohlgelernter giving him an
nie Banks baseball card.

The grave of the courageous Tova Perlow, the author's late aunt, who escaped from Poland
fore World War II.

The Perlow sisters with their mother. Most did not survive the Holocaust.

Rabbi Laura Geller officiating at Deanie Eichenstein's bat mitzvah

An Eichenstein family celebration

My own "field of dreams. Wrigley Field.

CHAPTER 8

THE WEDDING DANCE, CHASIDIC STYLE

R ita and I had been living together for about eight months before my parents finally met her. We never got around to planning the event. Instead it happened naturally and at the perfect location: beside my hospital bed.

After putting it off for a year, I had decided to undergo a hernia operation. During my last few months in New York I had moved furniture to make some extra cash. I got the hernia while hoisting a piano up four flights of stairs. I had taken the job because I was running out of money. Later, I learned that two stories had circulated among the extended family about why I was so broke. The most popular one was "Izzy's on drugs." My mom had a different theory—"Izzy must have given all his money away to the needy." The truth was less dramatic. I never took drugs, but I wasn't handing out dollars to street kids either. The simple fact was that although my parents sent me some money for room and board at college, they had no idea how much it actually cost to live in New York City. I didn't want to ask them for more, so I moved pianos.

I had gotten into the habit of letting weeks or even months go by without contacting my parents but I did tell them about the hernia operation. I was in my hospital room recovering from the procedure when Rita peeked out the door and spied a man with a fedora and trim grey beard walking down the hall accompanied by a lady in fashionable but very modest attire. Their arms were full of grocery bags.

"Iz—your parents," she whispered to me.

The sick-bed environment was ideal for our first get-together and the introductions went very well. I think it helped to rehabilitate my parents' opinion of Rita, which had become a little tarnished by the saber-tooth incident.

Shortly after we met, Rita gave me a carved jade saber tooth, which I wore around my neck. When I walked into my parents' living room wearing the green tooth, Mom and Dad had gaped at it in genuine horror. It might as well have been an actual tiger's tooth dripping blood. *Why is he wearing that? What does this mean?* was all over their faces but they didn't say a word. "It's a gift from Rita," I couldn't resist saying. After that, I figured that whenever Rita's name came up, they probably pictured her dancing around a bonfire with dozens of saber teeth swinging from her neck.

Rita, in real life, was much less worrisome. She was a girl from the neighborhood, after all, and her Modern Orthodox background was similar to my own in many ways. After my stay in the hospital, my parents decided that they ought to get to know Rita's parents. It was pretty clear to everyone that the relationship would end in a marriage, although we weren't yet ready to say that out loud.

Rita's parents and mine lived parallel lives but their paths rarely crossed. Their homes were four blocks from each other, a ten-minute walk. At the time, my father was rabbi of one of the largest non-Orthodox synagogues on Chicago's North Side. Rita's family, meanwhile, attended the largest Modern Orthodox synagogue, which was located directly across the street from my dad's. The Modern Orthodox congregants considered my father's synagogue *treife* and did not enter it. Dad based his services on the Orthodox prayer book but he used a microphone on Shabbat, and men and women sat together. Those two things alone were strictly forbidden by all Orthodox Jews, including the Modern Orthodox.

"I feel sorry for the Eichensteins," Rita's mother, Regina, told her once. "Rabbi and Mrs. Eichenstein are very devout, and yet because it's a *parnasah*—a salary—they're stuck with a membership that wouldn't know orthodoxy if it hit them in the head."

It eventually became a running joke between Rita's father, Dan, and my dad. "Rabbi, I've never met a group of people who know less about Judaism than the members of your synagogue," Dan would rib him. My dad would laugh because it was true. It's a testament to Dan's winning personality that he could get my father to chuckle about his own Talmud-deficient congregants. In addition to being gregarious, Dan Lipman had a brilliant mind. He was also the most persuasive human being I have ever met.

The two men hit it off instantly and so did our moms. When Dan and my father got to know each other, they became almost like brothers, and Regina became like a younger sister to my mother. When I asked Rita to marry me and we set a date—September 5, 1977—all four parents were already in position, like runners at the starting blocks.

"We'd better just stand back and stay out of their way," I told Rita.

"Why don't we get married at the park with our friends?" she suggested.

"That's a good one!"

We decided to let them have the wedding of their dreams for their children: in that community, weddings were everything. We had each other, we didn't need a wedding. So we let them have ours.

Within days of our announcement, Rita's parents had reserved a ballroom at the Palmer House, Chicago's finest and most opulent hotel. (Most Orthodox weddings take place at large hotels, which can accommodate the massive crowds). Now that there was an official engagement, both sets of parents could openly exult in their mutual good fortune. I assumed that my mom and dad had spent many sleepless nights wondering if I would marry an Irish waitress or an African-American soul singer. Gracious, beautiful, Modern Orthodox Rita was more than they had dared to hope for me. Rita's parents, meanwhile, felt as if they had hit the Orthodox jackpot. My father's synagogue may have been off limits, but the family line was impeccable. In that small world, marrying an Eichenstein was like bringing home the Duke of Windsor.

The guest list quickly ballooned to nearly five hundred. Knowing how difficult the logistics would be, Rita's parents hired a wedding planner named Phil to help orchestrate the event. The personality clash between the Lipmans and Phil was immediate. Unlike wedding planners of today, who go out of their way to please their clients and rev up the excitement, Phil was neither a people-pleaser nor jovial. Not exactly like the wedding planner from *Father of the Bride*, with the added insult of not knowing anything about Orthodox weddings, which are tightly scripted. Whatever Phil wanted to do, my in-laws wanted something else. They butted heads constantly, beginning with the invitations and continuing through every phase of the preparations.

Rita and I had very little say in the wedding plans, which was fine with us. The only time I intervened was when my father told me that he wanted his older brother, the Chief Rabbi of St. Louis, to officiate. I refused, knowing how the man disdained me. His back-handed compliment upon learning of my engagement was, "At least you married one of ours." There are very few people in this world I don't like—and they all happen to be in my extended family. This uncle topped the list. He was a prime example of intolerance and excluding those who are different. I disliked it then and dislike it to this day.

As the summer passed, my parents started to get nervous about Rita. Not that they didn't like her; they were very fond of my prospective wife. But Rita was ahead of her time. She was independent, not the cookie-cutter woman that most Orthodox men took as their brides. The Orthodox wedding ceremony is a long, extremely structured, minutely choreographed ritual. In the typical celebration, no one worries that the bride or groom will be tempted to step outside the bounds. But my parents knew that I was always outside their bounds and that Rita and I marched to our own drummer. Their concern started to swell into panic. What if Rita wouldn't circle me exactly seven times when she reached the *chuppah*? What if she pulled out a ring and handed it to me? What if she said something under the chuppah—recited some love poem or personal vow that she wrote? Orthodox law forbids the bride from uttering a word that is not part of the wedding text.

"Promise you won't say anything!" my parents pleaded whenever they saw us. By the time September arrived, Rita was ready to elope.

Rita's parents were anxious too. A few days before the wedding, we were at our apartment as usual. The phone rang and Rita answered it. A tense Regina asked, "Where are you? Why aren't you here at the house?"

"Why should I be there?"

"You need to come back now. You know why."

There's a saying about the Orthodox: they're more afraid of their neighbors than they are of God. It didn't matter that Rita had not lived at home for years. The night before a wedding, the bride is supposed to be at her parents' house so that she may emerge in the morning as pure as a spring rose. Rita shrugged, packed a small bag, and moved home for a few nights. She wanted her mom to be happy. She wasn't invested in having a traditional type of wedding, and this was her gift to her parents.

~~~

The Palmer House is a monument to luxury, the extravagant wedding gift of a Gilded Age magnate to his socialite bride. It houses one of the world's largest collections of Impressionist art as well as countless French antique furnishings, Tiffany masterpieces, cut crystal and garnet chandeliers, and a lobby featuring a soaring frescoed ceiling. Our wedding took place in the Grand Ballroom, which had dozens of arched doorways, gold sconces, a second-floor arcade that overlooked the room below, and a ceiling with so many levels of gold and cream crown moldings that it looked like an inverted wedding cake. Multiple chandeliers hung from ornate medallions encircled by swirls of gold filigree. When I arrived the day of the wedding, I felt more like an awestruck tourist than the star attraction.

Before an Orthodox wedding ceremony, a group of people who are close to the bride and groom converge in a separate room to watch them sign the *ketubah* or wedding contract. According to Jewish law, this contract must also be signed by two male kosher witnesses. In our case, a separate room had been secured for this purpose. As Rita and I pushed our way through the collected Eichensteins, Perlows, and Lipmans to the signing table, I saw my father glowering at my ultra-conservative brother-in-law. Mordecai had already commandeered the proceedings and was in the process of selecting the witnesses. As one after another of my friends stepped forward, Mordecai rejected them. He did the same with men from my father's synagogue. This one wasn't kosher enough—out! The next was not a strict Shabbat observer—rejected! On and on it went. No one wanted to start a fight over the witnesses and we were all eager to move on to the wedding, so we held our tongues and let Mordecai dismiss the volunteers like so many serfs. Finally he settled on two Black Hat males who passed his religious test and the ketubah was signed.

We shuffled out of the room and made our way toward the Grand Ballroom where I would walk down the aisle accompanied by my father and mother and then stand before the chuppah to await my bride. As we were about to enter the ballroom, I spied Phil, the wedding planner, leaning drunkenly against a wall. He grabbed my arm.

"Oh, man," he croaked. "I wish you luck marrying into this family. You're gonna need it." I sat him down on a velvet bench and that was the last I saw of him.

Mom and Dad took their places on either side of me and we slowly proceeded down the aisle. Mom glowed in a long dress made of layers of cranberry-hued chiffon. Dad wore a tuxedo with a wide, '70s-style tie. To my left, the hall was filled with women in sparkly gowns of pink, coral, gold, and blue. To my right, a sea of men in pale business suits. They were the members of my dad's congregation. Near the front sat a large group of black-coated men representing an army of ultra-Orthodox leaders.

I was staring straight ahead, trying to keep a stately pace, when I realized that my father was muttering something to me. "*Tshuvah, tshuvah.*" Repent, repent. What the heck? Was this really the time to chide me for past sins? According to the Talmud, God gives you an extra opportunity to do repentance on your wedding day because it's a new beginning. Maybe my dad was just making sure I was on track, but to my ears it sounded like a bizarrely-timed reprimand.

Up we went to the raised platform where a flower-entwined chuppha had been erected. We turned and saw Rita walking toward us, flanked by her mother and father.

She looked stunning. Her empire-style gown had an intricate lace-edged neckline and a ten-foot train, very glamorous. Behind the long veil that covered her face, I could see that she was beaming. When they reached the platform, Rita's dad stood behind me. "You can't back out now," he whispered to me jokingly.

Tshuvah, tshuvah," Dad was still intoning.

"You're in it for good. This is it!"

Tshuvah!"

Biting my lip so I wouldn't crack up, I stared straight ahead while Rita dutifully began her seven circles around me, trailed by our mothers, who held her train. The ritual pulled me out of my nervousness.

After my father gave the first part of the service, Mordecai called up seven men to give the seven wedding blessings. The first name he read was that of my uncle, the Chief Rabbi of St. Louis. So much for my request that he not be involved. Then my brother Yaakov approached the platform. A few more relatives. Finally, second to last, came Rabbi Shlomo Carlebach, who walked up along with his three-year-old daughter, Neshama. He rolled his eyes at us in silent solidarity and then sang the blessing in his beautiful tenor. As he left he whispered to me, "Brother, the big guns are here tonight!"

As soon as I had stepped on the wine glass and we were pronounced husband and wife, the room erupted into a celebration. We filed into the hotel lobby to wait for the ballroom to be reset with dinner tables for five hundred. Musicians played the traditional Chasidic tunes that warm my soul to this day. Women danced with women, and men with men. Rita and I were hoisted onto chairs and paraded around the room, an experience that's more thrilling than it looks, given that the people carrying you aren't exactly body builders.

Once the wedding feast was set up, the crowd settled in for dinner and toasts. As with the rest of the wedding, Rita and I had let the family decide who would give the toasts since they had a more passionate interest in it than we did. At one point, someone had told me that I needed to pick a religious man to toast us. I wracked my brain for someone who would pass muster with the Black Hats and selected Jack G., an acquaintance who was a little older than me and had longish hair. He was ultra-Orthodox, but I assumed he was not quite as strict as some other members of the community.

After Rita's aunt said a few words, Jack took his place standing directly behind me and Rita. I could feel his nervous energy as he directed his words to the row of stone-faced rabbis sitting down the dais from us.

"Izzy and Rita, we've shared lots of good times over wine and our families will share many more," Jack began.

"Wine is a unique affair: They say that people who have learned from older scholars—it's as if they have drunk rare old wine, as opposed to those who learn from their youngers and their peers, who drink sour grapes. Those of us who know Izzy well—and those who know him less well—may at one time have thought that he was more concerned about the length of his hair than the size of his yarmulke; that he was learning from the younger people and was caught up in the Pepsi Generation. Those of us who knew Izzy to have a musical appreciation that went from Shlomo Carlebach to Bob Dylan may have thought he was reluctant to appreciate the great *chazannim* [cantors] of old. Those of us who knew Izzy in New York, when his studies took him to Columbia slightly before his entrée to Lakewood Yeshivah tomorrow, or someday in the future—we thought of Izzy as having taken scholarship and academic cues from younger people. But it's not so. Izzy and Rita have had a *simchah* [celebration] tonight that is nothing less than a *Kibud Av V'Em* [honoring of their parents]. This *simchah* is part of a tradition that goes back hundreds and thousands of years."

Jack went on to praise Rita's family for their contributions to the Jewish community and to gush over mine for its scholarship and devotion to tradition. "This is rare old wine," he proclaimed. "And those of us who knew Izzy as a young vessel can resolve the conflict. May Rita and Izzy one day be as proud of all of us as we are of them."

Rita listened to all of this with a frozen smile on her face while I stared at my plate. It was an odd tribute: to refer to my mentors and friends as sour grapes; rib me about Lakewood Yeshivah, the Harvard of Talmudic study and the last place on earth I would ever be admitted or want to attend; promise the assembled Black Hats that "the conflict of Izzy is resolved"; and end by advising me and Rita to be prouder of the family. As Jack concluded his toast, I thought of the words from a Dylan song, "Positively 4th Street": *You got a lotta nerve to say you are my friend.* . . . Rita and I held hands and let the toast fade away on the larger, more benevolent waves of wedding cheer.

After dinner there was more revelry and the *mitzvah tantz,* a lovely ceremony where the bride dances with a long handkerchief. Rita performed this dance with my father and with a very exuberant Shlomo. Then Shlomo took the microphone and proceeded to serenade us for hours, leading the crowd in singing and dancing to all of his beloved music. It became a giant rock concert in our honor, with Jewish music, of course.

Suffice it to say that this was not your typical wedding. It was a blend of ultra-Orthodox (my family), Modern Orthodox (Rita's parents' friends), non-religious (from my dad's synagogue), and our collection of hippie friends. It somehow worked out and everyone had a great time. It might have been one of the first weddings in history where people from different Jewish persuasions celebrated together. But it was not to be the last.

After the wedding, Rita and I lived much as we had before. One big change did occur: Reb Shlomo asked me to be his full-time agent and I agreed. I left the radio station and booked him into venues all over the world—the United States., Israel, Europe, and South America. I did well financially as Shlomo was evolving into an iconic, almost mythic figure.

Meanwhile, Rita's parents and mine became even closer. My parents had been in a kind of social limbo for years because they were two very Orthodox people running a non-Orthodox synagogue. Rita's parents went out of their way to include my mom and dad in their social group. Their friendship lasted for the remainder of their lives. In fact, the two couples were so close that they are now buried in the same cemetery only about fifty feet apart from each other.

The combined forces of our parents made me uneasy. I knew that what we were really dealing with here was not in-laws or parents but future grandparents. Four future grandparents who were as subtle as earthquakes. They meant extremely well, but they were powerful forces. One of the reasons Rita and I had such a deep connection was that we both wanted our own lives. In the religious community, no one has his own life. It was clear that our parents were set on bringing Rita and me back into the religious fold before any grandchildren entered the scene.

Sometimes a single seemingly small event shines a brilliant light on everything around it. One day, when I had been married less than six months, I was walking along Devon Avenue not far from my father's synagogue. It was not Shabbat and I was not wearing a yarmulke. I saw my father walking down the street toward me and we greeted each other. Dad knew that I was not religious yet he was upset to see my bare head. It was annoying, but not exactly surprising.

Later Rita's father, who often came to my defense, called me at home to tell me that Dad had complained to him about the incident. "I said, 'Rabbi, your son doesn't need to wear a yarmulke twenty-four hours a day, even though you'd like him to.'"

"Thanks, Dan."

"Listen," he said, with his typical persuasive charm, "why don't you do what I do? Buy one of those Burberry caps just to cover your head."

I hung up and thought to myself, *This is never going to work.* Fundamentalist religious practice is like an oncoming train. It's not going to veer off in another direction. This one was going to keep coming straight at us unless we got out of Chicago. For the next two years, I looked for a way out.

Although I was doing well financially working for Shlomo, I knew I eventually had to separate myself from him. I loved the man but managing him was not what I wanted to do for a career. Rita's father agreed. And as far as he was concerned, he had the ideal solution. Dan Lipman would have loved me to go into the nursing home business with him. In addition to being a philanthropist and a big player in the religious community, Dan was a kingpin of Chicago nursing homes.

"There is tremendous wealth in the nursing home business, Izzy," he would remind me on a weekly, if not daily, basis. "You're interested in making money, am I correct? And you want to give Rita and your children a good life? Many people I have brought into the business are wealthy. Why shouldn't you and Rita and your children have those advantages?"

It was a nice offer and it would definitely have won me a lot of approving nods from the community. If you're married and you're not a Talmud scholar, the first question from everyone's lips is, "So what's your *parnose?*" What do you do for a living? "I run nursing homes," sounded very solid. I was tempted, but I knew it was not my identity. It didn't align with the "Let's do things our way" agreement on which our marriage was built. Although Rita loved her parents dearly, she was in my corner on this.

I kept my eyes and ears open for any escape hatch out of Chicago. It finally came the same way my radio job had, via the *Chicago Tribune*. A column that reported on entertainment in Chicago announced that a concert was being planned to celebrate the peace treaty that had just been signed by Egyptian President Anwar Sadat and Israeli Prime Minister Menachem Begin. This international event would be held in the Sinai and was being produced by Roger Vadim, the French filmmaker. A light bulb went on in my head. I called the French Consulate and told them that I represented Shlomo Carlebach and needed to speak to Roger Vadim about the peace concert. The consulate gave me his number (it would never be so easy today!). I called Vadim, identified myself and said, "I'm coming out to L.A. this week and I'd like to talk to you about helping to organize the event." He was enthusiastic about the idea.

I bought a plane ticket to Los Angeles. Within three days, I was meeting with Roger Vadim. I tapped every ounce of my considerable powers of persuasion to talk him into letting me run "The Concert for Peace."

"We're getting a budget together now," he said. "I don't see why you shouldn't head this thing up."

I walked out of his office, went to a pay phone, and called Rita.

"We're moving to Los Angeles," I told her. I knew she had trouble with cold weather and L.A. might be a place she would really like.

"We are? OK. . . . Great!" she replied.

"I think the best way for us to do this is for me to stay here. I need to start working on the peace concert right away."

"Right. I'll pack up," she agreed.

We gave notice to our landlady and I lived in a hotel in Los Angeles while Rita boxed up our belongings. She called her parents and told them very matter-of-factly that we were moving to California. They were philosophical about it and helped her pack.

My own parents reacted to the news calmly as well. In fact, they seemed relieved. I was an embarrassment to them and now they wouldn't have to make any more excuses for me. From two thousand miles away in Los Angeles, I listened for a tone of regret or pleading, but there was none. Six weeks after I had read about the peace concert in the newspaper, Rita arrived in L.A. and we began our new life.

CHAPTER 9

CALIFORNIA DREAMING

The Concert for Peace was just one part of what was going to be the International Peace Conference funded by the International Music Foundation for Peace. They must have had some wealthy backers because they booked a room for Rita and me at the Beverly Hillcrest, a luxury hotel in West Los Angeles with panoramic views of the city. Vadim's people assured us, "Just put it on your credit card. We'll reimburse you." (Everyone called him "Vadim," never "Roger" or "Mr. Vadim.") Plans for the concert were in full swing, twenty-four hours a day. Every night, usually after 10:00, someone would call and say, "We've got to meet right now! We have a new contact." The meetings always took place at a fancy Hollywood restaurant. I'd bring Rita along and we'd eat (charging it to our credit card) and plot the various aspects of the concert, which shifted daily along with the lineup of talent. My parents had no idea what was going on but Rita called hers regularly to report, "There's going to be a press conference any day now. You're going to be hearing about this!"

The concert was supposed to be held in October. On September 1, nothing had been solidified and we started to get the feeling that things weren't going well. We had been staying at the hotel for a month. That's when Vadim high-tailed it back to France. The International Peace Conference collapsed like a popped balloon and we were left with massive credit card debt from the hotel plus all our expenses.

It's not that we were naïve but we were young and we were from Chicago, where a person's word was taken seriously. I had totally bought the promises made by Vadim's people—a classic Hollywood story! I felt very disappointed about it at first, but eventually I let it go because the Concert for Peace is what got me and Rita out of Chicago. I viewed it as the price of my own "Operation Escape."

That concert ended up being my final job in the music business. Beyond wanting to branch away from Shlomo, the years I spent dealing with music people had convinced me that it was a flaky industry. The Concert for Peace debacle was the last straw. I was twenty-five and wanted to be able to give my family a good life, and that type of work couldn't provide enough security—plus I didn't like the vibes I was getting from the music world. When I told Shlomo that we had moved to California, he said, "Holy brother, I wish you well." Our business together faded away quietly like the last note of a song.

We found an apartment across from the CBS Studios on Beverly Boulevard near Fairfax in the heart of L.A.'s Orthodox community. Sometimes I wonder how our lives would have changed if we had landed somewhere else, like Santa Monica. I don't recall who directed us to the Fairfax area, but with all the kosher restaurants and markets, Jewish shops, and synagogues, it was a familiar setting in a very strange land.

Rita and I wanted to operate outside our comfort zone, and Los Angeles was the ultimate experiment. But now that we were here and the high drama of the peace concert was over, we felt shell-shocked. The people in our neighborhood weren't all that friendly. Where I grew up, I probably could have listed the occupants of every home within a five-block radius. Our isolation made this new city seem even more alien. The worst part was, we were broke and I was out of a job. At one point Rita went food shopping with our last remaining cash, a jar of pennies. The idea of calling our parents for help was totally out of the question—we would have eaten the pennies themselves before asking for a handout!

But there were a few definite benefits to living in Southern California. September was breezy and dry unlike the sweltering, sticky heat of Chicago. We loved the weather right away and started going to the beach and hiking in the Hollywood Hills. When the Cubs came to town we went to Dodger Stadium to cheer them on. I also joined the Actors Baseball League, which played every Sunday at nearby Fairfax High. The outfielder next to me was Bruno Kirby, who had played the young Mafia hit man Clemenza in *The Godfather II*. "Nice to meet you, kid. Keep your nose clean," he told me. I had no idea what he meant but he was a very nice guy.

We had been in the apartment only a few weeks when Rita's parents made their first visit. They were still highly skeptical about our choice of locale. "I'm glad you two have chosen to be orphans," Dan said in an amiable tone. "You come to L.A. Why in God's green earth you come to L.A., I don't understand—it's the craziest decision—but here you are. You have no friends. You have no family. You have no community. You don't know anybody."

Although Dan was hurt that we had relocated, he was also a devoted father and very loving and supportive of me. Above all, he wanted Rita to be happy. So he set out on a mission to find us some friends.

At that time, in the 1980s, there were still thousands of Holocaust survivors scattered around the world. Los Angeles was home to a large number of them, many of whom lived in our part of town. Everyone who survived the Holocaust was bound to all other survivors by their shared history and the psychological legacy of the experience. Wherever they lived, they supported one another. Both Dan and Regina were survivors. Dan's plan was to connect with other survivors in the Orthodox community and, through them, clear a path for us in Los Angeles.

Although she was a Holocaust survivor who had lost her entire family, Regina was not hardened or pessimistic. On the contrary, she was tremendously compassionate and open-minded. Out of all four parents, Regina was the most flexible and kindhearted. She had an independent mind and spoke it, usually without a filter. Where other people would have bitten their tongue, Regina loudly voiced any opinion. She was a breath of fresh air, and I loved that about her.

While Regina was imprisoned in Auschwitz, Dan had been living as a refugee in China, as part of Japan's Fugu Plan. According to some historians, the Japanese wartime government had created the Fugu Plan to attract Eastern European Jews to Manchuria, which Japan intended to conquer. The plan called for the Jews to contribute skills, brains, and money to the cause of the Japanese empire. The Japanese Consul General in Lithuania, Chiune Sugihara, courageously issued transit visas to Jews in Poland and Lithuania. With these visas, Sugihara was able to save thousands of lives. During the summer of 1940, when he realized that Jews who remained in Poland faced certain death, Sugihara spent eighteen to twenty hours a day writing the visas.

That summer Dan—originally Yedidiah Lipmanovicz—obtained a Sugihara visa and fled Vilna, Poland, with a group of yeshivah students. He traveled across Asia and spent six years as a refugee in China and another two in Japan before immigrating to the United States in 1946. Dan was the most charming, affable man you could ever want to meet, but occasionally a switch would turn and he would become critical. I don't know if it was a result of his experiences during the war or just a part of his personality, but over the years, I was stung by Dan's sharp words more than a few times, notwithstanding his tremendous generosity of spirit.

For Jews who survived the Holocaust, family became more than a focus of life. It was salvation. Scholar Sandra S. Williams writes:

"Re-creating a family and bringing a child into the world was a concrete attempt to compensate for their losses, to counter the massive disruption of their lives and to undo the dehumanization and loneliness they had experienced. . . . The children were often viewed as a symbol of victory over the Nazis. They were the future.[3]"

This was the case for Dan and Regina Lipman, and it was why my wife had been so sure that wherever she moved, her parents would follow.

All the Holocaust survivors I had known fell into one of two groups. Either they were completely committed to Orthodox Judaism or they were finished with it forever. Regina fell into the first group, which was surprising given the fact that she had been raised in a non-religious home. Yet after the Holocaust she embraced Modern Orthodox Judaism. It's not uncommon in any religion for people who were brought up in secular homes to go overboard when they convert, but Regina never did. She was a true believer and loved being Jewishly observant with her whole heart.

Many Holocaust survivors lost their faith in God and religion. Dan understood my misgivings about religion, which made me feel closer to him. But he expected me to shelve those misgivings and stay religious, like he did. He had expected it in Chicago, which is one of the reasons I left. Now, insisting that it was the best way to find a place in Los Angeles, Dan once again expected me and Rita to assume the attributes of a nice Orthodox couple. We were lonely, so we gave it a try.

During his first visit, Dan attended services at some of the nearby Orthodox synagogues. There were at least twenty-five from which to choose, eight on La Brea Boulevard alone. He selected two, a Modern Orthodox synagogue and one that was more conservative. Most of the congregants in both synagogues were residents of prosperous Han-

---

[3] Sandra S. Williams, "The Impact of the Holacauset on Survivors and Their Children," University of Central Florida, Judaic Studies Program, (1993). http://www.sandrawilliams.org/HOLOCAUST/holocaust.html

cock Park. Dan knew someone at each, so he wasn't a complete stranger. The plan was that Dan would be the icebreaker and introduce us to people. In addition to being charismatic, Dan was a masterful chess player, and he probably viewed this mission as not only a labor of love but also a fun challenge. Besides, he and Regina genuinely wished to be part of the Orthodox community in Los Angeles.

Every month or so, Dan and Regina would come to L.A., stay for a Shabbat, and attend one of the Orthodox synagogues, bringing me and Rita along. We tried to make friends with the people we met. But each Saturday afternoon, we would return to our apartment and say to each other, "I don't know. This is just not working."

There were lots of reasons we didn't fit in. The most obvious was that we had no money. The first question these people always asked us was, "Where do you live? North of Beverly or south of Beverly?" At that time, south of Beverly Drive was the wealthy area, while north of Beverly between Fairfax and Melrose, where we lived, was the poorer section. As soon as we revealed our address, our potential new friends would give us a big, fake smile and murmur "Mmmm." Their expressions would signal, *haven't made it*. It was as easy to read as a stop sign. It felt to us as if this community was all about status and money. Coming from the Midwest, we were not prepared for their bald-faced materialism. In Chicago, people who were wealthy didn't flaunt it. You could make friends up and down the social ladder.

Or maybe the difference was that in Chicago, whether I wanted it or not, I was very well known because of my name. The Eichenstein and Lipman families were prominent in the Jewish community, successful business owners, highly regarded religious leaders and educators. Until I got to L.A., I never realized how much my family name had influenced the way other people treated me. I may not have been a Talmudic star, but I was respected. When people found out who I was, their eyes either lit up or narrowed (if they knew about my rebel reputation). Either way, they cared. In fact, the extent to which people in my extended family had lambasted me for "not upholding the Eichenstein name" was proof of how much I mattered. In Los Angeles, no one knew the Eichensteins. It was like plunging from the penthouse to the basement, and I had to admit, it felt lonely to be an unknown.

Despite our "low" social standing and our uneasiness with the young Orthodox crowd, Rita and I kept trying to fit in. We had already crossed many lines that this group would never have condoned, such as living together before we were married. We didn't mention that. By never referring to large sections of our current and past life, we let them assume we were practicing Orthodox Jews. They may have been snobby and materialistic, but they took their religion very seriously. They wanted to study Torah. Rita and I were not even remotely dedicated to that. But we felt so lost in L.A. that we even tried a Torah study group—once. We continued to attend services at the two synagogues, having nothing better to do and wanting to support Dan in his sweet but doomed efforts on our behalf. But the devil is in the details—and Orthodox Judaism has a lot of details. I was destined to mess up somehow, and sure enough, I did.

I knew that Orthodox Jews were extremely careful about Shabbat laws. I had lived with those laws all my life until I began my slow retreat from that world. When I moved to New York City at the age of twenty, my extended family, there and in Israel, unwittingly shoved me the rest of the way out. Their relentless preaching about Orthodox Judaism and their outright contempt for me was so revolting that I said to myself, "This just can't be the truth."

Not driving on Shabbat is just the beginning of the restrictions. The Orthodox don't talk on the phone unless it's a medical emergency. They don't turn appliances on or off. They tear toilet paper into small sections and set it on the counter next to the toilet so that they will not have to do the work of tearing the paper off the roll on Shabbat. They tape light switches in the living room, kitchen, and bathroom to the "on" position before sundown on Friday night so that they won't forget and be stuck in the dark, because flipping a switch counts as work. If it is raining, they do not use an umbrella when they walk to services because opening an umbrella is work. I'm not trying to disrespect these rules. A lot of people live contentedly within their parameters. I just didn't believe in them anymore.

At the synagogue we attended most often, Dan had befriended a very wealthy and successful businessman. I'll call him Asaf. He was a hardcore, tough-nut Israeli who was strict in his Orthodoxy and unbending in his opinions. One Saturday morning, I went to synagogue and happened to stand next to Asaf. In the middle of the service, he turned his head and looked at me. His eyes dropped to my breast pocket, where he and I both simultaneously noticed a pen poking out. My heart skipped a beat in sudden embarrassment. A visible pen in my pocket, as if I could take it out any second and start writing! He glared at me. I glanced down, saw the pen, and got rid of it, jamming it into my trouser pocket. I knew it was all over; my Orthodox cover was blown. It was the last time I attended that synagogue.

~~~

My father-in-law's social strategy for us ultimately fizzled. We did make some acquaintances among the young Orthodox group but none that deepened into friendships. How close can you get to someone if you have to conceal the fact that you write with a pen on Saturdays? Or drive to the market? And we couldn't get used to the way the congregants spoke about other people—the belittling tone, the snide references to where this person worked or what kind of car that person drove. Since Rita and I were at the bottom of the pecking order, we knew they probably gossiped about us in the same way.

Dan's connections did eventually result in a job for me. One of the Holocaust survivors was the owner of an office supply company, and he hired me to be a salesman. As we shook hands to seal the deal, he asked, "How much should I pay you?"

"Pay me what you think I should get."

He offered $250 a week and we were thrilled to have it.

Rita was working on her MA in psychology (she would later earn a Ph.D.) and got hired to work at Thalians Mental Health Center at Cedars-Sinai, which was close enough to our apartment for her to ride her bicycle to the office. At last we were both working and could pay off the Peace Concert credit card bill and begin to think about the future.

Another thing that was going well was my relationship with my parents. We spoke at least once a week, and they always sounded delighted to hear from me. It was as if they had pictured Rita and me drifting around in a hot air balloon, and while they were very pleased that we had floated out of their territory, they had been anxious about the landing. Now that we were safely ensconced in a Modern Orthodox synagogue (little did they know how we felt about it) and I was gainfully employed, my parents were as satisfied with me as they had ever been. We were all relieved.

One year after our move to Los Angeles, I was still selling reams of paper and boxes of typewriter ribbon—selling the heck out of them, having doubled the volume of the company's best salesman within a week of starting the job. The owner was ecstatic and started urging me to mentor his son, a young guy who was a little entitled, a little lazy, and not very interested in the business that he would someday inherit. I talked with the son, but he didn't seem too keen on having me as his big brother.

At night after work, I researched various careers. I was trying to find something that was solid and steady yet could enable me to be financially independent. Equally important, I wanted a business that would allow me to be home with my family at night. My father-in-law frequently reminded me that a certain perfect job was still available in Chicago.

"You should have listened to me about those nursing homes," he'd say. "You know what the people who bought those homes from me are doing right now? They're laughing all the way to the bank while you're sitting here in this *farkakte* apartment on Beverly and Fairfax."

Dan pointed out that he could help me find a good job in Chicago even if it wasn't in nursing homes. He was frustrated and worried. Would Rita end up raising his grandchildren in a one-bedroom apartment with a view of the CBS parking lot? He had a powerful urge to protect us and keep us near. When so much of your family has been wiped out, you can be overcome by such urges, and that seemed to be what was happening with Dan.

Finally, about two years after our move, I honed in on a promising career. I had always been interested in real estate, so I researched the various types—residential, commercial, and industrial. What sector would be the most interesting? Where would I be most likely to carve out a place for myself? The answer was industrial real estate—warehouses and manufacturing buildings. It had the lowest percentage of practicing real estate brokers, so it would be easier to break into than the overcrowded residential or commercial fields. Despite cyclical ups and downs, real estate was a well-grounded business. I had been blessed with good people skills, and growing up in my dad's synagogue, I had a chance to encounter people from many diverse backgrounds. I had a strong feeling that if I put in my time and worked hard, I could expect to do reasonably well selling and managing these properties.

Dan approved of my career choice, although that was not the last time I heard, "You should have bought those nursing homes." It was years before he let go of that fantasy. Meanwhile, he ran my real-estate idea by some of his friends at the synagogue. At services one day, a survivor pulled me aside and told me, "You should think about changing your name."

"I should what?"

"Izzy Eichenstein is too ethnic."

"Thanks, but I think I'll keep it." I had to laugh at the thought of telling my parents that, from now on, they should call me something like "Ike Stone." The Eichenstein rebbes may have terrorized me like a gang of Talmudic gunslingers but the name was mine and I wasn't giving it up.

I started scanning the *Wall Street Journal* classifieds for real estate positions and went on a number of interviews. One firm, the M Company, kept calling me back. After a month of interviews, they hired me. It was an exciting time for me. Deep down, I had always wondered if I could measure up in the outside secular world. The owners, Paula and Jim, knew nothing about my background but they believed in me. They hired me over some MBAs and Wall Street types, choosing this ex-yeshivah boy instead. I was determined not to let them down.

When I handed in my resignation at the office supply company, the owner was extremely unhappy. He called Dan to deliver a parting curse: "I can promise you this: Your son-in-law will never make one deal in real estate!"

The M Company was a high-end, industrial real estate firm located in the San Fernando Valley, about a forty-minute drive from our apartment. I liked it from day one. Industrial real estate was completely different from anywhere else I had worked. It was a very detail-oriented business, yet just as important as the contract was your ability to negotiate with people. It was much more complex than sales, yet my skills in that area were what had convinced Paula and Jim to hire me over other applicants. As soon as I started working, both of them devoted a lot of personal attention to me. Jim was about fifteen years my senior and was the top industrial real estate broker in the Valley from the mid-1960s through the 1980s. It was an ideal place and time to learn the business. Three or four days a week, Jim would train me in contracts. Everything else about industrial real estate clicked with me and I picked up the nuances quickly.

Jim and Paula were devout Catholics. Many of their clients were Jewish. One of my clearest memories of that job was the time Rita and I went to their summer pool party. In a candid moment, Jim told me, "You're the first real Jew I've ever met." Some people would take that as an insult, but I didn't. I have no idea what a "real Jew" was in Jim's mind, but I believe he meant it as a compliment and that's the way I took it.

The "M" was headquartered in a building perched on a ridge in Woodland Hills that commanded a sweeping view of the Valley. I had been working there for about a year when my parents came out to see us. The highlight of their trip was a visit to my office. When I had told my father that I won the job over a slew of other applicants and later reported that I was already doing quite well at it, I could hear his pride and excitement over the phone. I knew why my success meant so much to him—in some ways it validated his own choices.

One reason my dad had originally taken his position as head of a non-Orthodox synagogue was that it came with a salary that allowed him to provide for his family. In the three decades since, my father had successfully negotiated two worlds: making a living while also tending to the spiritual needs of his congregation. During that time, the Eichensteins had regularly asked him for financial help. One of the things that most infuriated me about my family was that in addition to being hypocrites ("We won't work except to study Torah but we'll take what you earned"), all these years later, they continued to deride my father for his non-Orthodox congregation.

As well as donating to various Eichenstein relatives, my father was always trying to raise cash for my brother Yaakov's shul. Chasidic rabbis like Yaakov don't have a lot in common with rabbis who earn a salary. Their shuls aren't large temples but located in small commercial or residential spaces—in Yaakov's case, it was a rented storefront. But even very modest shuls need some sort of operating funds, and it fell to my dad to support Yaakov.

In light of all that, it's easy to see why Dad was so proud of how far I had come financially. I drove my parents out to Woodland Hills and watched a huge grin spread across my father's face when he saw the large sign over the entrance proclaiming the company name. My private office was luxurious, with paneled walls, picture windows, and a stately mahogany desk suitable for a captain of industry. Dad was beaming like a kid on his birthday. My mother stood beside him, smiling happily. I could practically read their minds: *Izzy's come back to the reservation! He belongs to a synagogue and he's got a prestigious job!* I was glad to be the source of so much joy.

~~~

Despite my nice office and the fact that I obviously had enough to eat, when my mother returned to Chicago she kept up a practice she had begun the first month we moved to L.A. Mom was a near-obsessive cook and baker, and she didn't let distance dent her desire to feed me and Rita. Whenever someone she knew was flying to Los Angeles, she would insist that the person bring us food. "Izzy, the plane is arriving at 5:45," she'd call to inform me, and I'd go meet the visitors in the baggage area to claim my care package. Mom would send sponge cakes (four at a time), rugelach, and frozen chickens. New pairs of underwear and socks would sometimes be wedged in between the chickens and cakes. After a while, Rita's mom started contributing her baked goods to the packages too. Once, while I was taking an especially cold and heavy box off the hands of my mother's latest courier, he gave me a look and said, "So they don't sell frozen chickens in Los Angeles?"

My mother and Regina were fast becoming best friends. In many respects they were smarter and more insightful than the two fathers about our decision to move. Both mothers were happy that we were out of Chicago. My mom knew, without ever coming out and saying it, that Rita and I were better off away from our hometown. They quietly encouraged us to spread our wings.

There was another reason my mother was glad I lived 2,000 miles away from Chicago. My brother Yaakov was becoming very powerful in the city's ultra-Orthodox circles, and he would have created a lot of conflict for my parents if I had been around. When I first returned to Chicago, he had already begun urging them to dress and behave more conservatively, and long before that, he had demonstrated how wary he was of the Chasidic elders who ruled his world.

For example, when Shlomo had bought me a ticket to Israel, my departure happened to coincide with the night Yaakov and his fiancée were meeting each other's extended families for the first time. A big dinner was being held to celebrate their engagement, and since my plane left at midnight, I planned on attending the dinner before going to the airport. Then Yaakov called and asked me not to come. "Your hair's too long." He was afraid my presence would ruin the *shidduch*—the match. I complied and left for the airport early. I met his fianceé's family a few months later when the engagement was already on record. They were perfectly friendly to me. Was my brother just being paranoid? It's hard to know. But one thing is for sure: I didn't reflect well on the family. I stuck out like a sore thumb with my long hair and faded jeans.

It wasn't Yaakov's imagination that having a nonobservant brother could stain his reputation in the ultra-Orthodox community. Such a stain could seep years into the future and affect things like who his child would be allowed to marry. As long as I stayed in California and my parents could report that we belonged to a Modern Orthodox synagogue, Yaakov was safe, and that made life easier for my parents.

Three years after Operation Escape Chicago, everyone was finally comfortable with how the family puzzle pieces were fitting together. Rita and I were still looking for kindred spirits to be friends with, but other than that, things could not have been better. It was time for the next step on our journey—starting a family.

CHAPTER 10

NACHIS FINDER KINDER
TEACH YOUR CHILDREN WELL

I n the summer of 1980 we found out a baby was on the way. We were thrilled and the two sets of future grandparents were ecstatic. Welcoming this infant into the world was an especially sweet milestone for Rita's parents because it signaled one more generation that the Nazis had failed to destroy—the tree of Jewish life branching out again. Once they heard the news, they started booking flights to Los Angeles even more frequently. Rita's mom took terrific care of her and wanted to savor this first pregnancy with us.

My mother and father were excited for us, too, and told us so whenever we called home. They didn't visit us often because the level of kosher observance in our house was questionable. Rita and I kept a kosher kitchen but not kosher enough for my parents. There are about eight degrees of kosher, and my parents and I were on opposite ends of the spectrum. When my mom and dad visited, they would nibble at fruit or sip some tea—it was crazy-making for me. The truth was, I was relieved not to have the pressure of them visiting.

We happily embarked on all the first-time-parent activities, like going to Lamaze class, where the woman learns how to do breathing exercises to make the delivery easier while the husband works as her "coach." Although I had misgivings about natural childbirth, Rita and I both felt that the breathing exercises would be good to know. A woman at our class told us about La Leche League, a group that espoused breastfeeding as a kind of holy mission. Natural childbirth, this woman said, was a crucial first step in the breast-feeding saga. The Lamaze leader implied that natural childbirth was far superior to using epidural pain blockers, which were probably being pushed by overworked obstetricians.

The Lamaze people weren't the only ones nagging us to go natural. Rita had been close friends with the daughter of Dr. M, a Chicago pediatrician famous for his opposition to medical breakthroughs such as childhood vaccines, which he said caused bad side effects. He, too, was a strong proponent of natural childbirth. Rita and I had visited Dr. M on several occasions when we lived in Chicago. He was a kindly man, the classic Marcus Welby–style family doctor until he opened his mouth to speak and turned into the Mad Un-scientist. "I no longer believe in modern medicine," he'd announce. "More than ninety percent of modern medicine could disappear from the face of the earth—doctors, hospitals, drugs, and equipment—and the effect on our health would be beneficial." He had thousands of followers, and they bought this stuff 100 percent. Conventional medicine may not have the cure for every disease, but this doctor's claim that it was basically worthless was radical. His hardline stance reminded me of my brother-in-law, the zealot.

Dr. M and his wife had been like surrogate parents to Rita while she was in high school. She later told me, "I guess I got an alternative education after all that time I spent in their house." When she learned she was pregnant, she called the doctor to get his advice. "Use a midwife," he said.

She wasn't *that* brainwashed. "I don't want a midwife. I want a doctor," she said, and ultimately we had our son at Brotman Hospital in Culver City.

Whether it's childhood vaccines, natural childbirth, or observing Shabbat, the all-or-nothing approach is kryptonite to me. It's the mark of a cult, and where there's a cult, reason goes out the window and people get hurt. That's why my children have heard me repeat my personal mantra a hundred times: "If you meet someone who says he has all the answers, run as fast as you can in the opposite direction."

David Abraham Eichenstein was born on March 7, 1981. We named our son after Rita's beloved Uncle Dave, who had brought her mother to the United States after the Holocaust, and after my father's brother, Avrohom, who had sponsored Rita's father so he could immigrate to this country.

Your brain gets rewired when you have a child. For Rita and me, that wiring wasn't only about our new roles as parents. It was the Jewish piece—how are we going to live? How are we going to raise him? Our forays to the Modern Orthodox synagogue had been more about trying to find friends than about religion. And then there were the grandparents. My mother and father enjoyed the long-distance illusion (encouraged by us) that Rita and I were happy Modern Orthodox campers. We had not told anyone how ambivalent we felt about it, although Regina and Dan had an inkling and did their best to help us ease our way into the community. All four grandparents were adamant that we raise our children as observant Modern Orthodox Jews.

March 14 was David's *bris*. It reminded me a little of our wedding—very crowded with people we didn't really know, many of whom were Eichenstein cousins who lived in L.A. but whom we had never met. We held the event in an Orthodox synagogue knowing that the Orthodox Eichensteins, as well as members of Rita's family, would attend. My Los Angeles relatives had not wanted to have much to do with us since our arrival, two years earlier, because of our reputation as irreligious hippies. When they came to David's bris they seemed surprised by what they found. I had a long cordial conversation with one of the older men, a very well-known L.A. rabbi. When we were done talking, he put a hand on my shoulder and said, "You know, you're not as bad as people make you out to be."

Now that we had a baby, Rita and I held out hope that the young Modern Orthodox crowd might be a little more welcoming. We thought if we got accepted into the group, maybe it wouldn't be so bad to live that way. "It's sort of a nice life," we told each other. "Let's give it another try at a different synagogue." We started attending services at Ohev Israel. The rabbi there was a former high school classmate of mine from Chicago and I liked his in-your-face style. He was an independent thinker and really gave it to that congregation, frequently challenging them, "If you're so Orthodox, why don't you move to Israel?" Eventually he, himself, moved to Israel, and some of the congregation moved there as well. Others who remained were relieved to see him go but I missed him. Rita and I had felt somewhat free to be ourselves around him—within (Orthodox) reason.

The good news was that the members of Ohev Israel, while a little cliquey, were much nicer than those at our former place of worship. It was a grassroots community of like-minded people who were mostly in their early thirties like us. In many ways, it felt like home: we all shared a similar background and all had been involved in B'nei Akiva, the youth group that was such an important part of my and Rita's teenaged years. The only problem was that we weren't Orthodox, and if we wanted to be accepted, we were going to have to convince these people that we were. Just like with our first synagogue, we had to carefully avoid driving on Shabbat or breaking any of the dozens of Sabbath-day rules, kosher laws, and other strictures that defined Orthodox life. If we did break those rules, we had to keep quiet about it, like covert agents. The cozy community feeling, the large and raucous holiday events, and having a place to go that felt, if not exactly tolerant, then at least familiar, seemed like a good trade-off for squashing our free-spirited instincts. For a while, maybe it was.

~~~

By this time I was starting to excel in real estate. I was going for my broker's license, having already earned my sales license. Salespeople are required to work with brokers and only allowed to do one type of transaction at a time (for example, sell properties or do mortgages) but brokers work under their own licenses and can conduct multiple types of transactions. Rita, meanwhile, had begun taking classes toward a doctorate in psychotherapy—a process that would take several years. I wanted to be at home as often as I could; the commute to Woodland Hills was beginning to frustrate me. Rita and I were debating the idea of moving to the Valley when a client made me an offer that solved the problem for us.

The opportunity came from a developer on the Westside. He had contacted me about buying a building in Chatsworth that the M Company was representing. I managed the negotiation, but in the end, the deal didn't pan out. However, this developer liked the way I conducted myself. A few weeks later he called again and said, "My partner and I are expanding our company—we want to assemble a group of industrial investment properties near the airport, LAX. The way you handled yourself during a deal that didn't work out was impressive. It says more about a person than how he handles a deal that *does* happen. For that reason, I want to hire you. I want you to be the guy who builds our real estate empire."

I was flattered, excited, and ready. I regretted having to leave the M Company, and they were sorry to see me go but they understood about the commute. I moved to an office on Century Boulevard near Los Angeles International Airport and started working for the developer, to whom I owe a huge thank-you. From 1983 to 1988 I helped him and his partner accumulate a great deal of airport-adjacent industrial property, all the while educating myself about the area. In 1988, I went into the business for myself and took out my own offices on Century Boulevard, where I work to this day. Best of all, I could now be home every night when Rita went to class or studied. Rita's mother was impressed: "I'm so grateful that you're supportive of Rita going to school and getting her career started." It was the sweetest compliment she ever gave me.

We were still living in the apartment on Spaulding Avenue, and it was getting too small for us. Rita started driving around to different neighborhoods looking for someplace to rent, and within a few weeks, she found a little bungalow at the corner of Canon Drive and Gregory Way. She didn't even realize it was in Beverly Hills. Two months later we leased that house, which we later purchased.

A few months after we moved in, Rita discovered that she was pregnant with our second child. Josh was born on November 14, 1983, in Cedars-Sinai Hospital where he and Rita got the royal treatment. We named the baby after my father's father, Rabbi Yehoshua Heschel Eichenstein, the courageous pioneer who emigrated from Russia in the 1920s and later became the Zhidachov Rebbe of Chicago.

My mother and father traveled to Los Angeles for the bris, which again was attended by many far-flung family members whom we rarely saw. Fifteen minutes before the mohel was about to perform the circumcision, my father pulled me aside and asked, "What are you going to name your son?" In the flurry of excitement and long-distance phone calls, I had actually forgotten to tell him.

"Joshua Heschel."

Dad paused, then calmly said, "You can't use that name."

"Why?"

"Because that's my father's name and you are not carrying on the traditions and ideals that my father had. I forbid you to use the name."

Tears welled in my eyes as I said, "Dad, this is what I'm doing. It's not your choice."

I'll never forget it as long as I live. It was another nail in the end of our relationship, if there ever really was a relationship. It's very difficult to love someone when conditions are constantly placed on that love. As I held my newborn son, I promised myself that I would never place conditions on my love for my children or for anyone else I let into my heart.

~~~

After Josh was born, we continued to socialize with the young families at our new synagogue but it was touch and go. When the rabbi we knew left to live in Israel, a lot of the congregants who followed him were people with whom we had been friendly. The new rabbi was a little more dogmatic, and the congregants who remained seemed to be growing more rigid. When we would get together at parties or holiday events, either Rita or I would inevitably let slip some hint that we weren't totally with the Orthodox program. Although we entertained often and people seemed happy to come to our house, we didn't get many invitations in return. As much as Rita wanted to connect with the other women, her way of thinking and questioning and being honest about her opinions seemed to get under their skin. Rita was never bound by the conventional rules that governed that world and it made some of the women nervous. We were different, and they could smell it.

In July 1986 we moved again. I found a house on a gorgeous lot in Beverlywood: a half acre on a cul-de-sac that backed up to Hillcrest Country Club. It was like a slice of the country in the middle of Los Angeles, particularly since the lot line blended into a heavily treed corner of the golf course.

The home and location were much more spacious than our bungalow on Canon Drive. When we told people at Ohev Israel we had moved and they learned the address, we instantly became Mr. and Mrs. Popularity. The big house in the cool neighborhood must have signaled to them that we were potential *machers*, and they temporarily eased up on their wariness about us.

I have to admit, it felt fantastic. There's nothing better than being part of a close-knit community of families when you're raising young children, and suddenly, Rita and I were at the center of this one—getting invited to Shabbat lunches, tapped to be on committees, solicited for our opinion about this holiday or that fund-raiser. At one point I was asked to serve as a board member. I said yes. When my mom called that week I casually mentioned, "I'll be starting on the board at Ohev Israel next month."

My mother was a very low-key person. She rarely raised her voice. Now she shrieked as if I had handed her a check from Publishers Clearinghouse.

"Oh, Izzy!" Her joy jumped right out of the phone. She covered the mouthpiece but I could hear her muffled shouts to my dad—"It's incredible! Izzy's on the board at Ohev Israel! Can you believe it?"

It was as if I was ten years old again and had miraculously aced one of the dreaded Torah tests. Why did this have to matter so much to her? Instead of feeling good I felt sad.

"I'm glad you're happy," I said. "I've got to go now. Bye, Mom," I hung up before she could pepper me with questions about all the marvelous duties I would be performing in my new role.

Soon my mother had genuinely good news to report to the family in Chicago: Rita was pregnant again. Both of the mothers responded by ramping up their food production. Regina instructed us, "You need an extra freezer. There's space in your laundry room. Get on the phone and have them deliver an extra freezer because I'm bringing food!"

Over the next several months the two mothers shipped, couriered, and carried a supply of precooked dinners, soups, sponge cakes, and cookies. Regina and Dan had bought an apartment in Los Angeles by then so they could be close to us and the grandkids, and whenever they flew in, they brought frozen home-cooked meals. Granted, the food didn't taste great after being frozen, shipped, partly defrosted, and finally cooked, but we ate it. They filled up the freezer, which we still use to this day. Our baby girl, Deanie, was born at St. John's Hospital in Santa Monica on September 16, 1987, and we had food to last us for a month by the time she arrived. Deanie completed our gorgeous family. The three kids were, and still are, the joy of our lives. All four grandparents were relatively young and healthy and there was room in our house for everyone. It was an incredibly happy time for us.

Seven years had passed since we had joined the Modern Orthodox community. Yet despite our recent popularity at Ohev Israel, we were still ambivalent about our religious devotion. It had not become easier; if anything, the effort was starting to suffocate us. The "day of rest" was the most stressful day of the week at our house. It got so bad that we'd make up excuses to take the kids to the doctor on Shabbat—"Their allergies are acting up!"— just so we could get into the car and drive somewhere. We felt totally imprisoned. Occasionally we would take the children to the park on a Saturday, feeling weird about it and looking around to make sure we weren't being seen by someone who could tell on us. "I feel like I'm in a straitjacket," I told Rita.

"So do I. But what are we supposed to do? Our parents. . . . " And we'd put off dealing with it for another week.

In April of 1988 we took the children to a Passover program held at a resort. It promised to be a lovely way to spend the holidays—we could indulge in rabbi-sanctioned recreational activities such as swimming and tennis while the children were cared for by hotel staff. There would be seders, services, and plenty of time to lounge around.

Late one afternoon, Rita was in our hotel room reading when I came in and sat down on the bed. I didn't say anything, just sat there lost in thought.

"Are you okay?"

"Rita, something just clicked. These people like this."

"What are you talking about?"

"It's just hit me. They're in this lifestyle because they like it. They're not just going along with it to carry on the tradition or to make their parents happy, like we are. They like all these rules. They like it!"

She nodded. "Their commitment is different than ours, that's for sure."

"Rita, we don't like it. Aren't you supposed to be in this life to do things you like, not to be told what to do? Why are we doing this? This is not us."

After all the strain and struggle to fit in, after the years of holding back the flood of who we really were, this two-minute chat is what broke the dam for us. The walls crumbled, the water flowed in, and we couldn't deny it or fight it any longer. We had to leave Ohev Israel and the Modern Orthodox community.

Many years later, Rita told me about another incident that happened the very week we returned from the Passover resort. We were still going to services; it would take more time to figure out what to do next and how to "come out" as non-Orthodox Jews. We were sitting in the Ohev Israel synagogue separated, as usual, by the wooden *mechitzah* that ran down the center of the sanctuary. It was about five feet high, so congregants could peek over the top and see the faces of the men or women on the other side. The rabbi was speaking about the *halakhah* of opening a can of soda on Shabbat. Did it count as work?

"I looked over and saw your expression," Rita recalled. "You looked nauseated. All the other men seemed contented, fine with this debate about a soda can. And you were in real pain. I saw the toll this was taking on you, and it made me so sad."

I was more than ready to put an end to the pretense, but I wanted Rita to understand what she would be giving up once we stopped playing the game.

"Listen, you know those invitations we get for Shabbat lunches?"

"Yes?"

"They're going to be gone shortly."

"What do you mean they'll be gone?"

"The minute it comes out that we openly drive on Saturday—and not just to the doctor—that we go to movies, that we do all kinds of things, those invitations are over."

"Izzy, I think this is your family paranoia coming out."

"If I'm wrong, I'll be the happiest guy in Los Angeles. But I'm telling you, it's over."

It happened within six weeks. We didn't make an announcement that we would no longer be Orthodox, we just stopped sneaking around and censoring ourselves. When people realized we really did shop and drive on Shabbat, nobody talked to us, nobody invited us over. The phone stopped ringing and our calls were not returned. The message was made clear one morning when Rita went food shopping at our local market and ran into a woman from Ohev Israel whom we considered a good friend. Rita waved and smiled across the vegetable bins. The woman stared at her for a brief moment, then turned her back.

We stopped going to services. We had been members of Ohev Israel for five years, had hosted large parties, and marched with the congregants at rallies. We had shared meals, prayers, holidays, and life events. We had attended services every Saturday morning without fail. No one asked us why we left: not the rabbi, not a single congregant. The silence was deafening. We even had a gift of jam returned to us—it wasn't kosher enough.

Looking back, my guess is that the people at Ohev Israel didn't ask why we left because they didn't want to know. Our leaving Ohev Israel was a rejection, and maybe they felt threatened by it. Rita was hurt but I had been expecting it. In fact, I had a lot of respect for the rabbi at that shul. Around the time we broke away, he told me that he was getting calls about us from all corners of the Orthodox world.

"They're asking, 'Why aren't you trying harder to keep them? It's a *shandeh*—disgraceful—that they're no longer part of the Orthodox community!' I tell them, 'Rita and Izzy are free to make their own decisions.'" The rabbi didn't ask why we left, but at least he didn't pressure us to stay.

Our parents did not take the news of our departure well. My mother and father had desperately wanted us to belong to that community, as my mom had demonstrated by practically levitating when I told her I was on the board at Ohev Israel. When they realized we were drifting away from that synagogue, the depth of their disappointment was communicated by their silence. They stopped talking about Ohev Israel, and our phone calls became even briefer. Rita's parents were equally dismayed, but they were around a lot more and were not the silent types. Dan voiced his objections but tried to temper his tone so as not to alienate us. They were unquestionably loyal to us, even though they were disappointed.

It wasn't as if we had decided to stop going to any synagogue, we just wanted to try one that was not Orthodox. Jumping from an Orthodox to a Reform synagogue would have been too radical for us, like traveling the distance from Florida to Alaska. Conservative was the logical next step. We decided to attend services at Temple Beth Am. I'm not sure what we were expecting, but we soon discovered that Conservative Judaism came with its own dogma and complicated rules. It was not "Judaism light." It was a total system of Judaic practice, and we weren't ready to buy into another program. We lasted only six months before bowing out. For the first time in our married life we did not belong to any synagogue.

⌇

Our oldest son, Dave, was a precocious boy who noticed everything and thought deeply about all of it. When he was seven and we were still active in Ohev Israel, Rita had taken him to a Peace Now rally at Roxbury Park, where American and Israeli activists were gathering in support of Mideast peace talks. Yael Dayan (Moshe's daughter), Betty Friedan, and Richard Dreyfuss were the featured speakers. Our synagogue was sending a contingent to march *against* the rally, holding placards that dismissed the speakers as traitors and drug addicts (Rita declined to carry a placard). At one point, Rita and Dave left the picket line and wandered over to buy a bagel at a table near the stage. They listened to Richard Dreyfuss talking about a two-state solution to the crisis in Israel. After a few minutes, David turned to Rita and said, "You know what, Mom? He's right." Our son was able to truly hear the viewpoint of others different from himself, which in my eyes was a very good quality.

When Dave was ready for grammar school, we enrolled him in H Academy, a private day school attended by the majority of Orthodox children in Los Angeles. Rita had visited every Jewish day school in the area—there were about seven of them—and analyzed them down to the smallest detail. H reminded Rita of the schools she and I had attended in Chicago. Boys and girls sat in class together until sixth grade. The curriculum was rigorous, with Hebrew and Judaic studies taught from morning until lunchtime and secular subjects in the afternoon. The families all came from similar backgrounds and most lived in the area, so it was easy to arrange play dates. In many ways it was a nurturing and secure environment for the children. The downside was that H was noisy, chaotic, and dirty—details we didn't really appreciate until Dave, and later Josh, were enrolled there.

Dave and H Academy were not a good match, but it was not really the school's fault, it was ours. We were changing. We never kept Shabbat the way the school taught the children to keep Shabbat. Even though the teachers told Dave not to worry about it, he was distressed by the culture clash. At home, we were a mildly observant family who kept a kosher kitchen and enjoyed many activities that nonobservant people did. On Saturdays, we attended the Modern Orthodox synagogue, except when we didn't and instead whisked the kids to the doctor's, stopping along the way to do "urgent" errands. Then we moved to a Conservative synagogue and then to no synagogue at all. Meanwhile, David's school was observant to the point where the boys were required to wear not only yarmulkes but also undergarments with fringed tzitzit beneath their school uniforms. If they were caught without these garments, even on the hottest days, they were admonished. By second grade it was obvious that David was very confused about the inconsistencies.

Rita again went to the different Jewish day schools, this time looking for a place where the curriculum and Jewish teachings would not conflict with our own evolving practice of Judaism. She zeroed in on a school that had not seemed Orthodox enough on her first tour: Temple Emanuel Community Day School. The moment she was finished visiting the campus, she called me.

"Iz, I have never felt better about a place. The kids are happy, the curriculum is creative, and the teachers are nurturing. They're learning about Judaism." We were both imagining how we were going to explain this to our parents. Although it was affiliated with Temple Emanuel of Beverly Hills, a Reform synagogue, the school itself was not strictly Reform and about 10 percent of the students were either Conservative or Orthodox. So as radical as it might look to the grandparents, we could still say, "The students are from all kinds of families."

We made the decision to move both Dave and Josh to Temple Emanuel Community Day School. Even more than our leaving Ohev Israel, this change of schools sent the grandparents into a tailspin. They weren't buying our arguments about the school teaching to all types of children. But we stuck by our vow to move the boys, and it was instantly clear that we had made the right choice. Temple Emanuel Day School was a free, open-minded, loving Jewish environment. Compared to H Academy, the Judaic studies were more alive and accessible. Both boys absolutely thrived there, and in June, when school ended, they, along with many other students, cried saying good-bye to their teachers for the summer.

It was because of the day school that Rita and I were introduced to Temple Emanuel, which was part of the Reform movement, the "ruined Judaism" I had been warned about all my whole life. We were between synagogues, having left Beth Am, and it was many months before we ventured into the sanctuary for services, but eventually we did.

Temple Emanuel of Beverly Hills—the name couldn't sound more affluent. Yet the congregation included many members who were of modest means, and with a few exceptions, even those who were well-off did not flaunt it as people had in the Modern Orthodox community. Right away, I noticed the congregation's lack of materialism and openhearted attitude. The synagogue's senior rabbi was Laura Geller, a visionary leader who was also one of the first female rabbis, ordained in the 1970s.

Rabbi Geller welcomed us warmly to our first service, which I clearly remember. Since then, I have talked to several other people who have ventured out of the Orthodox cocoon and made their way to a Reform service, and they all felt the way I did: as if I had walked into another religion. First of all, there was music—a guitar and a piano—unlike services at Ohev Israel, which were long on *halakhic* discussions and short on inspiration. There was less Hebrew and more English and the service was a bit shorter. The most startling difference was the emphasis on social action and trying to help the community at large, not just the insular community of Orthodox Jews. *This is going to take some time to get used to*, I thought, and it did. Yet from that very first Shabbat service, despite the strangeness of the experience, I felt like this was where I belonged. For the first time in my life, I could breathe freely. My asthma, which had plagued me for years, began to subside.

It was a long time before I consciously understood why Temple Emanuel felt so comfortable and right. It wasn't only that its openminded philosophy aligned with what I knew to be true about the world. It was also because I had sat with a similar congregation in a similar sanctuary hundreds of times, long ago, at my father's synagogue.

My dad's non-Orthodox congregation in Chicago was made up of the same welcoming, nonjudgmental people as those who attended Temple Emanuel. The members of Dad's congregation had doted on me and I had loved them. Forty years later I could still recite the names of half the congregation. Temple Emanuel's sanctuary, too, reminded me of my father's at A.G. Beth Israel. Its streamlined 1950s design, with walls of red brick and long windows of modern stained glass, could have been created by the same architect.

Most important, the sermons delivered by the rabbis at Temple Emanuel were similar to my father's sermons—and not just because they used more English and less Hebrew. These rabbis had an enlightened approach to Judaism and the Torah. They cared about social justice and loving compassion. My father's sermons had the same broad-minded perspective: Rabbi Moses Eichenstein had been highly regarded, even beloved, in the Jewish community for his soft-spoken, intelligent sermons, but most of all, for his tolerance. The only time that tolerance failed him was when it came to me.

My parents wanted me to be as devoted to Orthodox Judaism as they were. They didn't feel hypocritical leading a non-Orthodox congregation because they personally cleaved to the Orthodox laws. But they had been raised in that world and so had my older brother and sister. I had not. My father took his position as head of A.G. Beth Israel when I was only six. I wasn't inclined to be a rigidly Orthodox person anyway; it probably wasn't in my genes. But the fact that I was exposed at such an early age to the kind and open-minded members of my dad's congregation definitely nourished my natural tendencies. Unfortunately, my digression off the Orthodox path made my dad feel as if he had failed as a father. That's why he couldn't tolerate it.

At the time we joined Temple Emanuel, I had not put all these pieces together.

I was only conscious of one fact: I had been uncomfortable at every other synagogue in Los Angeles, and at this one, I felt comfortable. I knew I had been stuck. The world I was supposed to be living in was inflicting great pain. I was a spiritual person, and I did not think I was a bad person. I had to find a place of acceptance and a new worship home. It was scary to be in an unknown synagogue with a different worldview, one that members of my family would spit on. Yet within a few weeks it felt safe and familiar. When you feel safe, you can be emotionally and spiritually genuine. You don't surrender out of fear or weakness; you join with an open heart.

It has been said that there are two lasting bequests parents can give their children: one is roots, the other is wings. In fundamentalist families, a child's roots can be so heavy that his wings are not strong enough to lift him up. I had to trim my roots so that I could take off into my own life. I came to rest spiritually at Temple Emanuel.

CHAPTER 11

BEWARE AND BEHAVE

The landing at Temple Emanuel was a very gradual one. We were happy to send our children to the day school because they were thriving there, but the thought of actually joining a Reform synagogue brought on massive waves of guilt. For three years, we attended services at Temple Emanuel only sporadically and did not become members. Once a month, when Rita's parents were in town, we accompanied them to a Modern Orthodox synagogue called Beth Jacob. The sermons featured the same stifling righteousness and *halakhic* hair-splitting that had driven me crazy all my life, but having a place to go and pray on Shabbat was important to Rita's father and he was important to me. Dan liked mixing with the European immigrants who belonged to Beth Jacob.

Meanwhile, we got to know many of the congregants at Temple Emanuel whose children went to the day school. When we did attend services, we weren't strangers. The atmosphere felt fundamentally different than Beth Jacob—it was not as insular but also not as cozy; not as restrictive but also not as familiar. For all the flaws of the Orthodox community there were also positives, as Rita's parents pointed out. Maybe we didn't like that world, but, "Your decisions are not only yours—you are making these radical decisions for your children too!"

"They love it," we'd argue. "Dave's happy there. And remember, all kinds of children go to this school including Orthodox children. It's not a Reform school; it's broader than that."

"But not deeper," said Dan. There was no question that while the curriculum at Temple Emanuel was more creative and compelling for the children, it was not as rigorous as H Academy in terms of studying Jewish texts and traditions.

The constant needling by Rita's parents and the pointed silence from my mother and father on the topic of our children's education began to gnaw at us. What if they were right? The decision to lead a non-Orthodox life was the correct one for us but was it fair to deny our children exposure to their heritage? Were we rescuing them from a provincial, close-minded environment or depriving them of their birthright?

"It's okay to have choices," Regina pointed out, "but if you don't educate them, they won't really have a choice."

David had struggled at H Academy, not because of the curriculum, but because of the contrast between the Judaism practiced at the school and the more relaxed version we practiced at home. Now that he was twelve, maybe he should get another chance to decide for himself. Josh, who was nine, would go with the flow. He was a tolerant and laid-back child who wouldn't be bothered by the inconsistencies of different environments—or so we thought. Deanie would only be in first grade so she'd probably adapt. Children are resilient and flexible, we told ourselves. Five years after we had enrolled them in Temple Emanuel Community Day School, we pulled all three children out and enrolled them in H Academy.

To say that the grandparents were delighted would be putting it mildly. They tried not to make too big a deal out of it, probably worrying that they'd jinx it. Dan quietly congratulated us, saying, "You can't imagine how happy you've made me." My parents offered their warm appreciation and approval. Unfortunately, from the moment we signed the H Academy transfer forms, Rita and I started feeling queasy about it. But what did our "feelings" mean? Were we just projecting our own apprehension onto the children? We didn't trust our instincts anymore.

School started. On went the undershirts with the fringes, the white shirts, and blue vests for Josh and Dave. Deanie donned the navy-blue jumper and sky-blue shirt. We held our breath and jumped back in.

If the religious culture clash between our home and H Academy had bothered Dave in second grade, it instantly became clear that he felt even worse about it now. He hated the school and reacted to the Orthodox curriculum by grinding through it like a man tunneling out of Alcatraz. Ironically, the staff was very fond of Dave. The school principal was somewhat in awe of our Chasidic lineage and, as Dave told it, would show him off to visiting dignitaries. "He comes in with some famous rabbi and pulls me out of class and says, 'Look, we have an Eichenstein.' 'Ah, the Eichensteins! You're related to the Chief Rabbi from St. Louis!' It's hilarious."

At one point we were called into the principal's office and told, "Mr. and Mrs. Eichenstein, we're having a problem with your son, David. He likes the girls too much."

"Rabbi," Rita replied. "Would you prefer that he likes the boys?"

The principal didn't smile. "This is a place of study. Please remind your son."

Dave's acts of rebellion grew with each passing month. He bleached his hair blond. He got an earring. Rita's dad cornered me whenever he was in town: "You're not tough enough! You've got to discipline him."

"Listen to me, Dan. David is not the easiest child to raise. I can't get really tough with him because he's got two extreme parts of his personality: He's both very sensitive and very rebellious. If I crush his rebellious spirit by coming down on him too hard for this type of thing, I'm going to crush the sensitive part too. It's like walking on eggshells, but there's no other way."

Initially, Josh appeared neither repelled nor enthusiastic about the academic side of H Academy. His best friend attended the school and that seemed enough to make him happy. Josh was a strong and courageous spirit of a different sort than Dave or Deanie. He had a kind and easygoing nature; he also had uncommon wisdom beyond his years. Josh understood the predicament we were in and chose to conceal his quiet desperation until one day when Rita showed up at school early in the afternoon to drop something off. Josh ran up to her and begged her to take him home. The secular teachers later called us in for a meeting (without the rabbis). They told us it was clear to them that Josh was extremely unhappy and badly missed his old school. Why, they wondered, would we keep him in a place that made him so unhappy?

The final straw was Deanie. She had a joyous spirit and loving nature that made her instantly popular with both kids and teachers. However, the rules of Orthodox exclusivity and their rejection of those who are different extended even to six-year-olds. Deanie once innocently told her friends that our family had gone to eat pizza at a pizza shop that happened to be non-kosher. That was the end for her. From that point on, the other students made fun of her because she wasn't religious enough. Deanie would come home crying and tell Rita that they wouldn't include her in their games or cliques. Both Rita and I were tormented by the knowledge that we were forcing Deanie to spend every day in a place where she was taunted and excluded. Finally Rita confessed our dilemma to a school administrator with whom she had become close. The administrator's eyes grew wide when she heard we weren't Orthodox. "Rita," she whispered, "Your family is highly regarded here. For your kids' sake, don't tell anyone or they won't be treated well."

The whole debacle brought back memories of the years my parents had yanked me in and out of schools and summer camps. It made me ill to think that I was repeating the pattern with my own children. Deanie's tears and Josh's quiet stoicism broke my heart, and David had me seriously worried. Not only did he dislike H Academy, he was very aware of the pressure Rita and I were under to steer him toward becoming a yeshivah *bocher*. As the firstborn male, he got the brunt of our families' religious expectations.

Midway through the school year we could see David getting angrier and more stressed out. He could easily handle the intellectual load at the school, but the religious battering was taking a heavy emotional toll on him. Rita and I were like two tiny figures braced against an Orthodox tsunami that would pound Dave to smithereens if we couldn't protect him. We should have followed our instincts. After all, night after night we beat ourselves up about it.

The school year finally ended and so did our association with H Academy. Deanie and Josh returned to Temple Emanuel Community Day School. David had graduated eighth grade so Temple Emanuel was no longer an option for him. He was ready for high school, and he had already decided where he wanted to go: Windward, a secular private school. If he got his way, he would be the first Eichenstein male not to attend a yeshivah high school in the family's entire history—going back several hundred years. At least, the first that we knew of. There may have been others, but if so, they had been wiped from the family records. We were entering uncharted territory.

~~~~

Applying to Windward was a complicated process, involving school transcripts, teacher recommendations, entrance exams, and a personal essay. The school accepted about 20 percent of its applicants. David aced the tests and we set a date for the last hurdle, the personal interview.

When we had first put the children in Temple Emanuel, a hailstorm of negativity and anger had rained down on us. The family had pulled out all the stops, blasting us with arguments that would have impressed the Supreme Court. But now, beyond a few pointed remarks, Dan and Regina were uncharacteristically silent. They must have realized that if they wanted to stay in our lives, they were going to have to accept this. Dan and Regina loved our family—we were the center of their world—and they would never do anything to seriously threaten the relationship.

Dan always got the thankless task of relaying bad news to my parents back in Chicago. My own communication with them was minimal because I had no desire to tell them things I knew they wouldn't want to hear. Five years earlier, Dan had told them about the children's move to Temple Emanuel Day School. They had signaled their displeasure with silence. It now fell to Dan to inform my father that David was considering a secular high school. I expected the same silent reprimand transmitted by way of never mentioning the children's education during our brief, infrequent phone calls. But in the months before our final decision about Windward, my father's wall of silence cracked a couple of times.

A few years earlier, when he had retired from A.G. Beth Israel, my father had stunned me by publicly apologizing to me in his farewell sermon. In front of all his congregants he announced, "I regret not taking my son Izzy to ball games and spending more time with him. I made a mistake, and Izzy, I'm sorry." I was deeply touched by those words, as was everyone in the hall. Now, however, my father changed his tune. Dad called me as soon as he heard about David's application to Windward.

"You know what? The mistake I made was not bringing you up right."

"Dad, this is about David and what's best for him."

"Izzy! You have a coat, your yeshivah education. You have something to wear. If you don't give David the right coat, there's nothing to protect him, to keep him Jewish." There was real alarm in his voice, and I felt sorry for him, but my duty was to my son.

Late in the spring, David and I went to Windward School for our interview with the admissions officer. We had been told that she would spend some time with both of us, together, as well as a few minutes with each separately.

The woman was Jewish and in her mid-forties, extremely focused, articulate, and obviously bright. The interview with David went very well—his excitement about going to Windward outshined any nervousness he may have felt.

When we were finished with the parent/student part of the interview, the admissions officer asked, "David, do you mind if your dad and I speak privately for a few minutes?"

We walked outside to a little patio. What she said was the last thing I expected to hear.

"I want you to know where I grew up. I was born and raised in St. Louis."

St. Louis—the city where my least favorite uncle reigned as chief rabbi. So she knew.

"I hope you won't take this the wrong way," she continued, "but I think you need to make up your mind about how you want to lead your life. You have this beautiful son, David, and if you want him to live normally, be consistent."

Her bluntness surprised me but I knew exactly what she was saying. *You want to be an Orthodox Jew? Send him to an Orthodox school. If you're not going to live that way, we will happily admit him here at Windward. But it's time to decide.* She had seen David's transcripts and knew about the different schools he had attended; being from St. Louis, she understood about the Eichenstein family.

It all came down to one question: Was I going to repeat my parents' mistakes? Was I going to subject my children to the many overlapping neuroses I would probably always be dealing with—anxiety, fear of retribution and exclusion, confusion about where I fit in? Or would I free my sons and daughter to choose their own way of life, secure in the knowledge that I would love them no matter what? David was the most intense and sensitive of our children, and it was a shame that he was the one on the front lines of this battle. I could not mess his life up any more than I already had.

We couldn't waver any longer: we wouldn't survive emotionally. We wouldn't grow as a family. We wouldn't be happy. We had to make a decision, a *permanent* decision.

A few days later, David was notified that he had been admitted to Windward School. Rita and I had already agreed to make the leap. Dave would attend Windward in the fall, with our full support. The family would join Temple Emanuel. We would become official members of a Reform community.

~~~

The summer after David graduated eighth grade, we took the children to Israel, and I met up with Elli, my boyhood friend from high school in Chicago. Elli was now a reporter for an Israeli news station. My old friend had grown up to become ultra-Orthodox and also heavily into the Kabbalah, a branch of Jewish mysticism. Although he knew I was no longer observant, we were still close. I told Elli about the high drama that had surrounded David's application to Windward—that we had decided to allow him to attend but were still getting a lot of grief about it from the family and it was weighing on us.

"There's someone I want you to meet," said Elli. "He's a *chozeh*, and he's been a huge help to me." A *chozeh* is a seer—not just a wise person, but a mystic who has access to realms of knowledge beyond the physical plane. Rabbi Tzevi Hirsh Eichenstein, the founder of our family dynasty, had been a disciple of Rabbi Jacob Isaac, the famous "Seer of Lublin." In many Orthodox circles today, these seers were taken as seriously as they had been in the 1700s.

"Do you want to go talk to him?" Elli asked.

"Sure, I'm open to it."

The chozeh held court in a modern apartment on a nondescript street in Jerusalem. As we drove past, I could see people lined up down the block waiting patiently to ask his advice. We parked and joined them.

When it was finally my turn, I entered the apartment and found the chozeh sitting behind a large desk in a dimly lit office. Piled on the desk and stuffed into tall shelves were hundreds of Jewish holy books. The vibe in the room was warm and genuine. The chozeh did not accept money; his goal was simply to help people. He was a small man with a grey beard, dressed in the standard rabbinical garb. He gestured for me to sit and in perfect English said, "Do you have one question to ask me?"

"Rabbi, I want to confirm which high school I should send my son to. Should I send him to a Jewish high school or to Windward?"

The chozeh looked down, his brow furrowed and his arms crossed. He didn't ask me to elaborate. We both sat there silently while he silently meditated for what felt like ten minutes. Finally he said, "You should send him to Windward."

When I met Elli outside and reported the chozeh's advice, he was dumbstruck. It bothered him so much that he called the chozeh that night. "Rabbi, do you realize what you've just told my friend to do? Do you understand the ramifications?"

The chozeh replied, "Every person has his own path in life."

In the end, despite all the *mishegas*, Rita's parents dealt with our decision graciously. Were they happy about it? Absolutely not. But they adjusted. They never attended services at Temple Emanuel with us, but occasionally, I still went with Dan to Beth Jacob. Temple Emanuel Day School was known for its theater program, and Regina had a background in the Yiddish theater in Chicago, so she loved to go and watch the plays and musicals.

Sometimes Dan would join her. By this point, with sad resignation, he had accepted the situation. Dan's health was beginning to decline and he was, no doubt, saving his strength for his last long battle.

Dan Lipman had a great heart. He was kinder to me than anyone from my own family, and I was much closer to him than I was to my parents. We had some heated arguments, but when he was on dialysis the last seven years of his life, he called me every single day. In spite of all our disagreements about how religiously we should raise our children, I loved my father-in-law dearly and I know he felt the same.

As for my mother and father, they never mentioned the exodus from H Academy or our joining Temple Emanuel although, of course, Dan told them everything. My parents and I never had one discussion in which the words "Temple Emanuel" were uttered. If they or my brother or sister asked where I went for the High Holidays, I'd just say, "I went to a shul in the area." For my family, joining Temple Emanuel was absolute blasphemy. It was literally a curse word, way beyond their window of tolerance. Often, I wished I could have been open with them, but my desire to preserve the slightest thread of a relationship with them superseded my need for honesty.

When we became full-fledged members of Temple Emanuel, the friends we had already made there never knew what a life-changing decision it was for us. In fact, they didn't know anything about our background. Many years earlier, Rita had convinced me not to talk about our families with the people we met in California, even those in the Modern Orthodox community. I had forced myself to keep quiet but it wasn't easy. I never could mentally escape my history, and I had a compulsion to confess it and explain it to everyone. Staying silent felt like a lie of omission—these people would assume I was just like them, but I wasn't. Still, I knew Rita was right. If we did talk about our background, it would define us and color all our friendships.

I had no route, no atlas or GPS for finding my way out of Orthodox Judaism and into Reform. Nobody was going to advise me and tell me what my options were. Many nights I lay in bed wishing things were different. I wanted to give my kids a normal life with an extended family of loving cousins, aunts, and uncles, but it wasn't meant to be.

We eventually found our footing at Temple Emanuel, and we never doubted that we had done the right thing, but it was always bittersweet. There were many people at Ohev Israel whom I liked a lot, and I still feel a great sadness that those friendships were not allowed to continue.

The people who shunned our family after we stopped observing the Orthodox laws have no idea how much pain they caused. They have done tremendous damage to us and other families like ours and they should be held accountable. There is something very destructive about the way Orthodox Jews in America and Israel deal with former members who love being Jewish but have chosen a different path. How can any of us grow if we can't listen to and learn from one another? What message was sent to my young children when friends who once invited them over for Shabbat meals suddenly vanished from their lives? I never asked any of our Orthodox friends to change the way they observed, how they lived or ate, where they prayed, or where they sent their children to school. Why, then, was I judged and excluded?

Although my father did not practice tolerance with me, he did with his temple members, and I credit him for teaching me my live-and-let-live attitude. Thank God that, in the end, I had the presence of mind to pass it on to my children. From the first day David walked through the doors at Windward, his behavioral problems disappeared. We didn't openly discuss it, but by sending him to that school, I let him know that he was free to choose the life he wanted. Dave understood my unspoken message: "I love you. I apologize for your having to go through the turbulence of the religion and all the family craziness. Now go figure out who you are and may God be with you."

David has told me many times, "Windward was the turning point where my life became normal. It was the best thing that could have happened to me. Without you taking a stand, we all would have turned out so differently."

He blazed the trail and has been so successful in his life. Josh and Deanie suffered slightly less. Josh went to Beverly Hills High where he flourished. He was able to play baseball for the team there and ultimately played for the Israel Baseball League. He is a grounded and wise young man, flourishing in life on his own path. Deanie went to Windward, where she thrived socially, academically, and in theater. She has the rare combination of an independent mind and a spiritual nature. She, too, is happily pursuing her own path.

Josh and Deanie were shielded a bit from the unhappiness my upbringing caused me. My parents' visits to California were rare, and beyond that, our communication was extremely superficial. What is the middle road between angry silence and estrangement? Indifference? The best term to describe our relationship would be "Don't Ask, Don't Tell." If I told my parents anything beyond the most bland, insignificant news, they would disapprove and I couldn't handle that. In turn, they didn't want to acknowledge any actions of mine that they would feel duty-bound to criticize. There wasn't much wiggle room in our détente.

When our children were little, we used to travel to Chicago several times a year and see my parents there. All three kids have fond memories of those visits. We would stay at Dan and Regina's large home which was only a few blocks from my parents' house. From there we would walk to my parents' place, past my father's former synagogue, A.G. Beth Israel. My dad and mom could not have been nicer—my mother fussed over the children and cooked them special meals and treats. They had only one rule: the boys had to wear yarmulkes in the house. My father was the gentle, tolerant, and wise man his congregation had adored. David, Josh, and Deanie loved to spend an hour or two a few times a year with their Chicago grandparents.

After David became bar mitzvah, we stopped going east so frequently. But when he was fourteen, I took him to New York to attend a family wedding. It was the first time he was old enough to notice how unusual the scene was. All the chief rabbis, in their long beards, black suits, and enormous fur hats sat in a row on a raised platform sourly scanning the crowd. Everyone else fawned over them like serfs before the lords of the manor. As we stood to the side watching, David whispered, "You know what? Without the violence, our family is like the *Godfather* movies."

"You've got that right," I said. *Violence isn't always physical*, I thought to myself.

Somebody once asked me, "What do you think when you look back at everything you went through with your family?"

A phrase sprang into my head. "Torah over everything. Keeping *halakhah* takes precedence over tolerance of others. That's the way it is in an Orthodox family. Torah comes before people."

I wanted to be a different type of parent to my children. I wanted to be an open thinker, to be flexible, to be accepting, not to bully or shame them. I wanted to be a consistent guide in our confusing world, and I hope they know that if I lost my bearings a few times, it was only because I am still finding my own way, too.

CHAPTER 12

FINDING MY "LOST" FAMILY

W hen you are a child, connection is all that matters. My life, early on, was about looking for love, finding the road blocked, and not knowing where to turn. Sports and my teammates were the closest I had to a family. Until I met Reb Shlomo and moved to New York, it was impossible to avoid the company of those who saw only my faults. As I got out into the world and more people related to me positively, I began to respond differently. The vibe and environment dramatically changed and I began to value myself.

If you're shot up with religious propaganda every day of your formative years, it stays in your system. It took me years to overcome the trauma of my family's rejection and their "Torah-true" lifestyle. It has only been within the past decade that I have warmed up to Jewish prayer and Jewish learning; it was always too painful to re-enter that atmosphere. But—and this is the part my family will never understand—I happen to love being Jewish. I just had to find a way to be Jewish without being Orthodox. I never hid my Jewishness. I never ran from it. At my Reform synagogue I am accepted for who I am. I don't have to pretend to be devout in a way that doesn't ring true for me.

Like many fundamentalist groups, my extended family played a game of pretend—pretending that my dad's synagogue didn't exist and pretending that children like me who veered off the Orthodox path—didn't exist. Both ultra- and Modern Orthodox communities still play that game, and if anything, it's worse today than it was back then. Rita, who became a psychologist specializing in childhood learning disabilities, has encountered Orthodox parents who pretend their child's disabilities are not real, even if the kids suffer only from a mild case of ADHD. It's not that these parents don't want to help their children. It's that they know how the Orthodox world punishes those who deviate from their version of normal. The parents worry that if their child has an actual diagnosis, it will compromise his or her marriage prospects.

I knew from a very early age that I didn't fit in to my family's Orthodox world. The fact that my dad was the rabbi of a non-Orthodox synagogue that was sneered upon by his family complicated the situation. I was an adored "clergy kid" in my dad's congregation but a Torah-challenged rebel in our Orthodox family. In both settings, I was expected to be on my best behavior at all times, especially in public.

As an adult, I have met other grown-up "clergy kids" who have experienced some of the same things I have. "You live on an island encircled by religion," was how one man put it. His father was a Pentecostal minister who traveled around the United States with his family spreading the Gospel. Whether your dad is preaching to a country church with twenty worshipers or to a massive congregation in the city, you are always held up as an example. The pressure is constant. That's why so many clergy kids act out and become rebellious—they want to run away from the limelight, to express themselves, to be like everyone else.

Not all clergy kids run wild and reject their communities. There's so much to lose, and many of them are happy to stay on their familiar island. As far as I know, I am still the only Eichenstein in my generation to leave the Orthodox fold. From what I've seen, clergy kids who stay in their religion tend to become more steadfast and inflexible the older they get. Those who find the courage and willpower to leave end up being spiritual in a different way. They take what is meaningful from their past and blend it with what they discover on their own. The ones who have really moved on have a deep appreciation of other faiths and understand that there are many ways to express spirituality—different truths, different holy books, different leaders.

These people—call them defectors, free thinkers, or rebels—pay a tremendous price for their questioning minds because in all fundamentalist groups the rebels are eventually cut off. In my case, I found another community and Rita and I had our own family. But it was as if I had no extended family. I always prayed that one day I would find just one family member I could relate to and have a common bond with. I couldn't believe I was the only person who had felt confusion and doubt about our religion. It was a lonely world with all family doors shut, but I couldn't sell my soul for approval. Then, one afternoon at a bookstore in Los Angeles, my prayers were answered.

~~~

I was in the biography section when I noticed a new release, *Spiritual Radical,* by Edward K. Kaplan. The book's subject is the late Rabbi Abraham Joshua Heschel, whose mother and my (maternal) grandfather were twins. Rabbi Heschel, who passed away in 1972, is considered one of the great Jewish philosophers of the twentieth century. He was a prominent advocate of the civil rights movement, and marched with Reverend Martin Luther King, Jr. Much of Rabbi Heschel's childhood in Warsaw, Poland, was spent at the home of my grandfather, Rabbi Alter Israel Shimon Perlow, the Novominsker Rebbe of Warsaw, after whom I am named. My mom was Heschel's first cousin.

As I skimmed the book, I noticed that it had a drawing of my family tree with the names of my mother and her many brothers and sisters. One name caught my eye— Gittel (Tova) Montheard, the eldest of the twelve siblings. *Who was this?* Mom had never once mentioned that she had an older sister named Tova.

Thinking back on it, I recalled overhearing a relative whisper something about a Tova Perlow who was unaccounted for after the war, but it was unclear who she was. What had happened to her? The family tree noted that she had died in 1956. Did she have kids? For heaven's sake, this was not some distant relative, this was my mother's oldest sister, an aunt that I knew nothing about. I immediately purchased the book and took it home.

Reading the names of my mom's sisters and brothers, most of whom had perished in the Holocaust, was wrenching. I stared at each name, asking the questions that can never be answered. How did such things happen? Where was God while all this was going on? Growing up in the post-Holocaust Jewish community, there was always an undertone of profound sadness and loss. We children were educated about the Nazi atrocities and when we looked at our parents, teachers, and cousins—all of whom lost countless family members or entire families—the scars were everywhere. Some of those scars were numbers tattooed on the skin of survivors of the death camps. Other scars revealed themselves in the broken souls we all met in our community. Why some had the courage and fortitude not to hate or keep on hating is a testament to how amazing the human spirit can be.

My mother was never in a camp. She had been sent to London during the war before the final darkness fell on Poland. Mom would never speak of how or why she was saved or describe her escape to England. She was an incredibly loving and sensitive person and tears always seemed to be welling up inside of her. The tears were from a broken heart that never fully recovered from the profound losses she always carried with her. My mother died in 2002, and memories of her sister Tova must have passed into eternity with her along with all the other secrets.

I scoured the Heschel biography for information about Tova and learned only that she had been living in Paris when she died and was married to a man whose last name was Montheard. The next morning I called directory assistance in Paris and asked the French operator, "Can you give me the phone numbers of all the Montheards in Paris?"

"You may have three numbers," she replied in stilted English. Only three! I jotted them down.

I dialed the first one and struck out. The person had never heard of Tova Montheard. The second number was the winning lottery ticket. A Mrs. Montheard answered my call and listened to my carefully prepared story. Luckily, she spoke English. Within a few minutes she interrupted.

"Oh! You must be referring to my ex-husband's grandmother, Tova, who was the daughter of a famous rabbi in Poland. You should call my ex-husband, Philippe Montheard."

With my heart pounding, I dialed Philippe. For the first few minutes he refused to believe my story, but as I filled in the details, he finally decided, "You might be telling the truth." He gave me the phone number of his father, Jean Pierre, who was Tova's son. My first cousin!

We bonded instantly. In that first phone conversation Jean Pierre related the life story of his mother, the sole known religious defector, other than me, among four generations of Eichensteins and Perlows.

Tova was the oldest child of our grandfather, the Chief Rabbi of Warsaw, and she was considered brilliant but she had nowhere to go with her curiosity and her bright mind. In Poland, at the turn of the twentieth century, there were no schools for Jewish girls. Tova had a great desire to see the world, and knew she would have no opportunities to educate herself if she stayed in Warsaw, so sometime between 1900 and 1910 she broke free. She ran away—first to Palestine where she got married and then divorced—a rare and shocking event at the turn of the century. There is no way to confirm it, but Jean Pierre believes that, by then, his mother was cut off from her father and family. From Palestine, Tova journeyed to Paris, where she fell in love with a Frenchman who was not Jewish. He kept her safe from the Germans during World War II. After the war ended, Tova attended university and graduated from the Sorbonne. Later, although she no longer was a practicing Orthodox Jew, she taught and wrote about the Talmud. Tova had two children, Jean Pierre and Katya, who both stayed in Paris. Katya had passed away, but she had children—second cousins to Dave, Josh, and Deanie.

Jean Pierre and Katya had enjoyed a normal childhood complete with the extended family of their French father. However, aside from one distant relative, nobody from the Perlow family would have anything to do with them. Jean Pierre had not known we existed and was overjoyed to finally connect with his new-found first cousins.

For me, Jean Pierre and his family were an amazing and completely unexpected gift. I was elated at the prospect of having cousins I could just hang out with and be myself. About six months after I contacted Jean Pierre, he and his wife, Andree, came to Los Angeles and stayed at our house. They were as fascinated by our shared history as we were.

By this time, my father was in his nineties and had mellowed in his attitude toward me. He was still living in the family home in Chicago along with my sister and her husband. They had moved in before Mom passed away. On the eve of my mother's funeral, I found my father sitting in the bedroom, his head in his hands. "Can you imagine the state of my life right now? Mom is gone and I'm stuck with this situation in the house." If anyone could imagine how bad it would be to share a roof with Miriam and her rabid, right-wing husband, it was me. I felt really sorry for Dad.

I wanted to ask Dad in person what he thought about my new-found branch of the family. Shortly after my French cousins' visit to L.A., I traveled to Chicago.

"Dad, I want you to know that I found Mom's oldest sister's family in Paris."

"Really?" He was surprised but not astonished. "Maybe you should come with me into the den."

Dad's den served as headquarters for the exchange of classified Eichenstein information, which he guarded like nuclear codes. When he had something to tell me, he would call me in there, shut the doors, and draw the curtains. Now, after he had secured the room, he sat down while I remained standing in front of his desk.

"Tell me about the family."

"Here's what I know. Mom's oldest sister had two kids, Jean Pierre and Katya. Jean Pierre married Andree, who is one of the nicest people I've ever met. She's the daughter of a Vietnamese diplomat, speaks perfect English, and knows the family history inside out. She isn't Jewish, so none of their children are Jewish. Jean Pierre's sister—Tova's other child, Katya—ended up marrying a Jewish man and her children are quite religious."

Dad was quiet for a moment, absorbing the information. "Sit down," he said, sighing. "The idea that Mom's father, the Chasidic leader of Warsaw, has grandchildren who aren't Jewish is beyond my comprehension." He didn't say it with sadness and he wasn't angry at me for delivering the news. He was simply stunned by it.

That was the one and only time we talked about the French family. I concluded from Dad's response that he had always known about Tova, if not her children. My sister's reaction confirmed that she, too, was aware of Tova.

"Oh, yeah. I knew that one of Tova's children was very Jewish-oriented." Typical of Miriam, the only piece of the story that mattered was the part relating to Judaism. My brother Yaakov was even less interested. "Don't talk to me about them. We're not proud of that side of the family."

In 2007, Rita, Deanie, and I traveled to Paris to visit our cousins. Jean Pierre, Andree, and Philippe hosted a welcome party for us, taking over the top floor of a restaurant and inviting all their relatives, as well as some of their friends. Among the guests was Katya's daughter, Muriel, a physician. Shortly after that dinner, Muriel took us to meet her father, Katya's Jewish husband. He was an artist and woodworker, and at the end of the evening he took us upstairs to his studio. There he showed us an old photograph of my mother as a girl of about fourteen, surrounded by her sisters. It was one of the few items from her childhood that my aunt had carried with her throughout her life. Muriel's father had enlarged the photograph and crafted a beautiful frame for it. He presented this to us as a gift.

Tova and her sisters will always be part of our family even though I never met them. Her children and grandchildren have become the extended family that we are closest to. We call and email each other frequently and visit one another every few years. Jean Pierre, my son Josh, and I have a strong physical resemblance.

The last time Rita and I were in Paris, I visited Tova's grave. I wanted to spend some time with my long-lost comrade, my one and only co-defector. I thought about how much of my life's energy had been spent trying to overcome my particular set of hurdles. It had been grueling, yet my struggle paled in comparison to the war, exile, and terrible losses Tova had suffered. At her graveside, I said a prayer for Tova Montheard and thanked her for the family she created.

~~~

My father had been a supremely healthy man for eight decades but around the time of my discovery, he became ill. Our relationship had been superficial for at least twenty years. The last time I had attempted to have a discussion with him about life, philosophy, or religion was when the children were still young. My parents were visiting, and I was curious about Dad's opinion of *When Bad Things Happen to Good People* by Rabbi Harold Kushner, which had just been published and was at the top of the bestseller lists. His book explored how tragedy affects people's faith in God.

"I read Kushner's book and really liked it," I began.

"Don't talk to me about that book. He doesn't believe in a personal God." My father launched into a five-minute tirade about the author until I held up my hand—*"Fine, I get it"*—and left the room. I vowed to myself that I would never again discuss anything meaningful with him and I kept my promise.

It was frustrating because I knew that with others, my father could be quite open-minded. His sermons had been legendary for their insights about how to live an ethical life in a society that was going through immense cultural shifts during the period Dad had his pulpit: the 1950s through the 1980s. When he was in his twenties and thirties, Dad had often attended lectures by scholars and philosophers of all faiths and backgrounds. At A.G. Beth Israel, he obviously enjoyed exploring a wide range of topics in his sermons. He was free to welcome anyone into his home and to behave in the kind and tolerant way that was his natural inclination. As he had confessed to me when I was a teenager, he would have been a psychiatrist if he had not been compelled by tradition to become a rabbi.

The proof to me that my father had a secular streak was his lifelong friendship with a man named Paul Lang. Paul was an intellectual who taught history at a public high school and also was the principal of the Hebrew school at my dad's synagogue. He and my father talked on the phone every day except Shabbat. Neither Paul, nor any of the people my father dealt with on a daily basis, were religious, and there is no doubt in my mind that he thrived on the oxygen of the non-Orthodox world. The people in that world loved and respected him in return.

For much of my life I couldn't understand why my father, who was so beloved by his congregants for his tolerance, was so unbending with me. Why, even after I was an adult, did his normally open mind slam shut on a topic like the Kushner book? I finally figured out that no discussion about a heretic like Kushner could be allowed because Dad thought I'd take it as a sign that he condoned my defection. To his children, he always had to play the role of the strictly Orthodox parent.

A few years after the Kushner incident, Dad let slip a rare acknowledgment of our mutually unsatisfying relationship. He had been chiding me about the children's education again.

"Listen to me, Dad! I can't be who you want me to be," I shouted.

He bowed his head briefly. Then he said, "I'm the son of a Chasidic rabbi. I can't change who I am, either."

Once Dad became ill, I began to approach him differently. I couldn't forget everything that had happened between us, but I longed to connect with him, somehow, while I still could. Over the last two years of his life I called him every day. His caretaker told me that Dad always lit up when he heard me on the phone. During each call, I would sing him one of the Chasidic melodies he had taught me when I was five years old. At Friday night Shabbat dinners, when guests from our congregation had often joined us at the table, I was the one Dad asked to sing the Shabbat tunes that were dear to him.

Near the end of my father's life, I visited him with David, who was then in his twenties. Although his illness had severely limited his ability to speak, Dad asked for a picture of David, I like to believe that he wanted us to feel loved, or maybe he wanted to make up for the craziness of my upbringing and the pressure he had put on Dave about school. I happened to have one of those wallet-sized school portraits parents carry around forever. I pulled it out and gave it to Dad, and he slipped it into his shirt pocket and pressed it to his heart.

CHAPTER 13

CLIMBING MT. SINAI

My father passed away on December 31, 2007, at the age of ninety-five. I was not asked to speak at his funeral. It was five degrees in Chicago on the day of the service. Josh, Deanie, and Rita accompanied me to the ultra-Orthodox synagogue. The chapel was filled with hundreds of men in long beards and black hats. My brother and cousin both spoke and then, to their later regret, they called a man named Richie to the lectern.

Richie had been a boy of fourteen when my father took him under his wing. I had already been sent away to Pittsburgh by then and Richie's dad had recently died.

My father became a surrogate dad to Richie, who grew up to be one of those rare scholars who can converse brilliantly on both secular and Jewish subjects. I wish I had a transcript of the eulogy Richie gave for my father. He described Dad's broadness of mind and eagerness to learn from all sources. He recalled how my father loved talking about his youthful excursions around Chicago to listen to prominent thinkers such as Emma Goldman and other philosophers of the day. He quoted members of Dad's congregation who revered him for his welcoming and nonjudgmental spirit.

When we went back to the house where we were sitting shivah, my normally passive brother was still seething—"I was so embarrassed by Richie's speech!" he said. Rita and I just shook our heads.

In the years since Dad's death I have often thought about how different my life would have been if my family could only have acknowledged all that my father accomplished at A.G. Beth Israel. They never gave him the stamp of religious approval he craved. If the family had appreciated how beloved my father was—if they could have been tolerant of him as he was of his congregants—then maybe my dad could have been more tolerant toward me. But everybody in the family lined up against him. The relentless judgment from the extended family, including my brother and sister, affected him deeply. He knew how they felt about him and had a heavy heart because of it.

Growing up, the atmosphere in my house was always very strict and serious. If there had been a sign on the front lawn it would have said, "Beware and Behave."

Despite our fraught relationship, I know my father enjoyed my ability to lighten the mood and contribute some levity to our home. And even though he turned on me at crucial times, it was also obvious that Dad admired the way I stood up to the family. He knew that the elders did not respect him yet he lacked the strength to defend himself or cut loose from them. My father was stuck in no-man's-land. Most rabbis join an association—Orthodox, Conservative, Reform; they all have affiliated groups. My dad did not belong to any of them. He couldn't. He didn't know where he fit in.

Ask anyone in the Orthodox community and they will say that their predictions about my father were right. They'll say Dad did a lousy job of raising me and the proof is that I fell off the way.

~~~

It's Memorial Day weekend 2012 and this year the Jewish holiday of Shavuot is on the same weekend. Shavuot commemorates the day when God gave the Torah to the Jewish people, every one of whom was assembled at Mt. Sinai. Memorial Day and Shavuot have a lot in common. Both are an opportunity to stop and give thanks to those who have died for the cause of freedom.

It's Sunday morning. Some people are going to church, Jews celebrating Shavuot are going to synagogue, and many are going to the cemetery to honor those who have fallen. I will be going to my very early softball game and then I plan on racing over to Temple Emanuel, where I will participate in the memorial service and liturgy known as *Yizkor*, which is recited four times a year. The service is led by the rabbi and cantor and includes prayers for loved ones who have passed away. This year I will remember so many—my parents and in-laws—and those who fought for this country.

It's just after 7:00 a.m. and I'm wearing my baseball uniform. I have a change of clothes in the car so I can dress appropriately for the service, which will be held about twenty-five miles from the baseball field. I am nervous. When I was growing up, playing a baseball game on Shavuot was strictly prohibited. Although I am more than fifty years old, I am still trying to connect the dots of my identity. Going to my baseball game is not exactly climbing Mt. Sinai to receive the Torah, but Jewish tradition says there are at least seventy ways to acquire the wisdom of that holy book. We each must find our own way up Mt. Sinai. Who appointed a select few to decide who and what is holy? Where does a grab for power by religious leaders overlap common sense and the common good? I still mull over these questions every day.

As I drive to my game I am haunted by the scorn my ultra-Orthodox family would direct toward me for playing ball today. I still can see their searing expressions of disapproval, but I must confront my personal demons. I hear Dad's voice in my ear, *"So this is what it has come down to. On a Jewish Holy Day, a day when God gave our people the holy Torah, you are about to get behind the plate and be the catcher for your team."*

"To thine own self be true," I say out loud. That was one of Dad's favorite mottos, and the irony is not lost on me. But my neurosis starts to take over and I think, *"This will be a terrible game. We will lose, I will play poorly, and the revenge of the family will be wreaked upon my body and soul."*

As always, the propaganda plays in my head like nonstop elevator music. But I am determined to stay on my path, to keep confronting my own demons, and to find my own way up Mt. Sinai.

I get behind the plate, put on my catcher's gear, and say to myself, *"The heck with all that stuff. This is who I am. I am playing to win not only the game but also to win by being true to myself. Let the chips fall where they may."*

I look around at my tribe: my teammates, a great bunch of guys. I am catching Lew, our all-star pitcher. At first base, I have red-light Dan, always hitting in the clutch when the game is on the line. I see Jeff at second, a superb hitter with great fielding skills. We have Anthony at shortstop, a young player with blazing speed. At third, Don, top-notch with an all-around A-plus game. In left field we have Ari, our hardnosed captain, who hates to lose so badly that he would run through a wall for the team. In center there's Daniel, a powerful young newcomer. Brad is in right field playing on sheer guts, with a partially torn ligament and still leading the way with clutch RBIs throughout the season. Missing today are Matt, our all-star left fielder, our regular first baseman Roger, who each week serves up a great defensive play or a timely hit, and Frank, our left-handed clutch hitter.

We fall behind 6–0 then we fight back, cutting the lead to 6–5 by the third inning. By the fifth we lead 8–6, then in the sixth we fall behind 10–8. In the bottom of the sixth, we take the lead for good and win the game. It feels great, a terrific team win clinching a playoff spot. The demons lose.

I rush to the car and change into my synagogue clothes. The Sunday traffic is light and I quickly drive from the west San Fernando Valley to Temple Emanuel, getting to the service just in time. Right before Yizkor begins, the rabbi gives me the honor of raising and then holding the Torah scrolls during the entire memorial service. I am tired from catching a full game and my arms ache but my weariness fades as I hold the Torah.

The rabbi speaks movingly about how, as we grow older, many of us speak through our thoughts or dreams to those who are no longer with us. As the Yizkor service unfolds and the prayers are recited, I thank my parents for what they gave me. I treasure being Jewish on my own terms. I thank those who are no longer here, who fought the battles that gave us the freedoms we enjoy. As I sit there holding the holy Torah, I give thanks most of all to God who is helping me on my personal journey and who put so many wonderful people in my path. They have helped light the way as I search for my own route up Mt. Sinai. Then, as the service concludes, I remember that the First Commandment is "Believe in G-d." It is not "Believe in your family." We are all created in G-d's image and we are all standing on Mt. Sinai together.

A LETTER TO HEAVEN

Dear Zaide,

Thank you for having the courage and the foresight to leave Europe in the 1920s. You preserved an entire generation. What did you see that led to your exodus out of Chodorow, Russia? The rabbis there were steadfast in their refusal to allow people to emigrate. They could have saved millions of lives. Yes, many Jews who immigrated to the United States stopped being strictly observant and yes, many lost their Judaism altogether. But does that justify the rabbis' blindness to the darkness descending upon Europe?

Zaide, you were a rebel for leaving Russia. Some of us end up being rebels not because that is our intent but because we must go our own way, find our own path. Those who have walked that road learn that it is fulfilling, it is full of adventure, but it can be quite lonely. I did feel like a sinner and an outsider. What would you have advised me to do?

Let me ask you, Zaide, is there really only one way to pray or practice? During the Depression years you had an early Shabbat *minyan* before people went to work. That shows your deep compassion and understanding of how changing circumstances must influence the way we live and worship. I, too, believe that real spiritual growth comes from developing yourself with the guidance of religious principles, not from being controlled by those principles.

Are we separated in heaven by how much Torah we know or by how we treated our fellow human beings?

Here on earth there is an expression, "What doesn't kill you makes you stronger." I think that is a ridiculous statement. Yes, you can survive but it will probably weaken you, dilute you. Religion that practices tough love ostracizes those who question. It destroys their self-esteem. When you destroy a person's self-esteem, you extinguish their gifts and kill off who they are. They become a shell of the person they might have been. To me that is a true sin.

Do you think I am wrong?

AFTERWORD

In life we all make choices. Choices have consequences. In our home we had Shabbat candles lit every Friday night, and the blessings over the wine known as the *kiddush* were also always recited. My wife and I were happy that our children's friends were always comfortable enjoying a Friday night Shabbat meal at our home, the Jewish traditions were not forgotten; they were for the most part honored and yet . . .

On a beautiful sunny day in June 2010, I had the honor and the privilege of celebrating and participating in my son's joyous, interfaith wedding to a terrific girl, who is beautiful, unique, funny, and charming. After almost being destroyed by suffocating dogma, I promised myself that my children will have the freedom to choose their own path.

A grandson of a rabbi descended from the great Chasidic masters marrying a Catholic girl from New Jersey, a match guided by love not by credo, not exactly the master plan for having Jewish grandchildren. How they will be raised is not up to me, but simply put if being crushed by dogma was the price for having Jewish grandchildren, I refused. Life many times can deliver a menu full of conflicts along with experiences that would be hard to dream up.

A short drive away from this idyllic setting in New Jersey, where my son's interfaith wedding took place, sit many of my very close cousins and nephews who are studying at one of the world's foremost yeshivas. They will be great Talmudic scholars and future Ultra-Orthodox Jewish leaders. The distance between my son's wedding in physical miles to where my cousins and nephews pored over the Talmud was very short, but the distance in the differing lives cannot be measured.

No one has really has the answers to life's deep questions, so I will close this book with a quote from another scholar from New Jersey, a musical scholar, Bruce Springsteen, with my slight modification to his lyrics. "Show a little faith, there's magic in being the real you, none of us have all the answers, but hey you're alright and oh that's alright with me."

To know you are all right is to know you are loved and accepted for who you are. . . . My father did say, "To thine own self be true."

GLOSSARY

apikoros/apikorsim   heresy/heretic; one who negates the rabbinic tradition

Baal Shem Tov   charismatic founder of Chasidism and its first leader in Eastern Europe

bar mitzvah   term denoting both the attainment of religious and legal maturity as well as the occasion at which this status is formally assumed for boys at the age of thirteen plus one day

beit midrash   study center; study hall

B'nei Akiva   Zionist youth group

bris   circumcision ceremony

Chanukkah/Hanukkah   annual eight-day celebration, called "The Festival of Light," commemorating the rededication of the temple in Jerusalem by Judah Maccabee after its defilement by Antiochus of Syria.

Chasidic/Chasidim/Hasidic Judaism   a branch of Orthodox Judaism that promotes spirituality through the popularization and internalization of Jewish mysticism as the fundamental aspects of the Jewish faith; those that follow this branch of Judaism

chazannim   cantors

chevrusah   partnership; students at yeshiva typically study this way.

chochom   a high-achieving learned person

chozeh   a seer—a mystic who has access to realms of knowledge beyond the physical plane

chuppah/huppah/chuppa   canopy, symbolic of the house, under which a wedding ceremony takes place

daven/davening   to pray, praying or leading prayers, often with strong swaying from the hips.

d'var Torah   a speech about an aspect of the week's Torah portion that had personal significance, usually given by yeshiva students

farkakte   lousy; screwed up; washed up

gelt   money

halakhah/halakhic   Jewish law

Kabbalah   a branch of Jewish mysticism

ketubah   wedding contract

kibbutz/kibbutzim   (Hebrew word for "communal settlement"), a unique rural community; a society dedicated to mutual aid and social justice

machers   influential people

mashgiach   a supervisor whose role was to provide a positive influence and maintain Torah standards for students, such as in yeshivas

mazel tov   good luck

mechitzah   a separation used in synagogues to separate the men from the women

mishegas   craziness, madness

mitzvah tantz   a ceremony where the bride dances with a long handkerchief at the wedding

mitzvot   the 613 commandments that Orthodox adult males are expected to follow, including prayers three times a day as well as an increase in dailyTorah study

Modeh Ani   the morning prayer

mohel   the man who performs ritual circumcisions according to rabbinic regulations and customs

Nachis Finder Kinder   teach your children well

parnasah   a salary

parnose   livelihood; living

peyes   long side curls

rebbe   rabbi

Rebbetzin/rebbetzin   rabbi's wife

rosh yeshivah   the head of the yeshiva

rugelach   cream cheese cookies, usually made with filling

Shabbat   sabbath, which lasts from sundown on Friday to sunset on Saturday

shandeh   a shame

Shavuot   a harvest festival, but it also commemorates the revelation at Sinai and the giving of the Torah

shidduch   match, marriage, betrothal; arranged marriage.

Sim Shalom   the weekday blessing

shivah   Jewish mourning period of seven days observed by family and friends of the deceased

shtibel   small house of prayer used by Chasidim

shtreimel   large, drumlike fur hats worn by the ultra-Orthodox

shul   synagogue or temple

simchah   celebration; party

talmud chochom   a high-achieving Torah-learned person

tefillin   two small, black leather boxes with straps attached, that contain passages of Hebrew script. The boxes are strapped on (one on the head and one on the arm) by Orthodox Jewish men each weekday morning.

treife   non-kosher

treife medinah   an "impure" country

tshuvah, tshuvah   repent, repent

tzitzit   the fringes at the corner of a prayer shawl.

tznius   modesty; ultra-Orthodox imposes these rules on its community

yarmulke   skull cap

yeshivah   a school of high Talmudic learning

yeshivah bocher   a yeshiva student; a gullible or inexperienced person.

Yisroel   Israel

yizkor   prayer for commemorating the deceased

Zaide/zaide   grandfather